Katharine McDowell Hunley

Innside Nantucket

By Frank B. Gilbreth, Jr. and
Ernestine Gilbreth Carey

CHEAPER BY THE DOZEN

BELLES ON THEIR TOES

Innside
Nantucket

FRANK B. GILBRETH, Jr.

Illustrated by Donald McKay

THOMAS Y. CROWELL COMPANY : NEW YORK

Sixth Printing, December 1954

MANUFACTURED IN THE UNITED STATES OF AMERICA
BY THE VAIL-BALLOU PRESS, INC., BINGHAMTON, NEW YORK

Foreword

This is a true story of the adventures of my brother, Bob, and his wife, Barbara, in operating a resort inn on Nantucket Island, Massachusetts. All of the material was furnished by them, and they are the co-authors. Since Barbara was the focal point around whom the inn revolved, while Bob went to school teaching on Nantucket, it seemed logical to present the story in the first person, as related by Barbara.

The names of all characters except members of Bob's and Barbara's immediate families are fictitious. If the names happen to coincide with actual names, that's a coincidence. But the characters themselves are real—and characters.

F. B. G.

Contents

Contents

I ~ Bridegroom with Two Loves

"The steamer will be docked in eleven minutes, Barb," Bob told me accusingly, "and you're not even dressed."

Standing there dripping onto a wet towel, in front of the kitchen sink, I was so obviously not even dressed that there was no use trying to deny it.

In fact, in addition to Bob, two of our paying guests could testify that I was not even dressed. They were the guests who, ignoring with jolly informality a sign on the door, had come bouncing into the kitchen for ice cubes a few minutes before—and then had beat a hasty, if open-eyed, retreat.

I have never been fond of sponge baths, even when enlivened by games of peekaboo with members of the immediate family. Now that complete strangers had entered the game, I was frankly on the verge of throwing in the sponge.

"I'm doing the best I can, Bob," I choked. "Instead of trying to rush me, I wish you'd do something about that kitchen door."

During the week that we had been operating Anchor Inn on Nantucket Island, Massachusetts, I had been urging Bob continuously to put a lock on the door. But he maintained—and with some justification—that we had to rush in and out of the door so often a lock would slow us down. Besides, we hoped to have a bathtub of our very own, *some day*.

In lieu of a lock, Bob had put three different signs on the door. First he had tried "Private." Then, when that didn't work, he tried "No Admittance." Finally, when *that* didn't work, he tried "Positively No Admittance."

"I'll add," he said agreeably, as if there was no extreme to which he would not go to satisfy my slightest unreasonable whim, " 'This Means You.' "

I don't want to give the impression that I was standing *September Morn* fashion—or "mothuh nekkit," as they say on Nantucket—on the towel. Actually, to cling tightly to what little modesty I possessed after a week of kitchen ablutions, I was clad in a rayon slip. The slip seemed as intent on clinging tightly as I was.

Fortunately, too, I received some additional camouflage from thirty or forty wet sheets, pillowcases, and diapers. We had had fog for four days. Since Bob hadn't been able to dry the laundry in the yard, he had hung a small portion of it from overhead pipes and temporary clotheslines in the kitchen.

I took refuge behind a sheet and attempted to dry myself with one of the wet towels. The few remaining dry towels had to be saved for the guests.

"Don't give up the slip," Bob suggested.

I had no intention of giving it up, even though I had to go through some unladylike contortions to keep the slip down to

2

knee level, while sliding the towel up to my back and shoulders.

"Nine minutes to go," Bob announced after consulting his watch. "We can just make the boat, if you get a wiggle on."

If those remarks were meant to evoke even a dry chuckle from me, all I can say is that they failed miserably.

It didn't take me long to get dressed, because I was too tired to care how I looked. It had been a long day, and Ann's first birthday. Bob and I had managed to devote ten minutes, at lunchtime, to the ceremony of lighting a single candle on a store-bought cup cake. Ann ate some of the cake and, later, all of the candle.

I had spent the rest of the day doing my even-tempered best to be a gay young mother, while watching Ann; scrubbing seven toilets, seven bathtubs, and seven sinks; cooking nineteen breakfasts; making twenty-one beds, and dusting and vacuuming eleven rooms. I had also cooked lunch and supper for Bob, Ann and me, and had typewritten five letters answering inquiries received that morning about reservations.

Bob, meanwhile, had been cutting the lawn, unstopping a sink, wrestling with a mountain of laundry, answering the telephone, answering the front door bell, providing ice, and toting suitcases upstairs and down.

Mercifully, Ann was asleep now, on a pillow in a wicker basket in our bedroom. We *did* have both a bedroom and a toilet we could call our own. But no sink—except for the one in the kitchen —and no bathtub. Although it was now eight o'clock at night, the kitchen sink was still loaded with the morning's egg-hardened dishes.

It seemed a special sort of irony that in the first house Bob and I had even owned, and a house which boasted seven lovely bathtubs, we had to do our bathing in front of the ancient, soapstone kitchen sink. This wasn't so bad for Ann, who could still fit into a dishpan. It apparently wasn't so bad for Bob, who professed not to mind sponge baths. For me, it was misery.

I've always liked to stretch out full length and relax in a tub, with steaming water all the way up to my nose and soap bubbles exploding luxuriously in my ears. A sponge bath, standing on a moist towel while stretching over to wet a washrag from widely spaced faucets—one of which spattered ice water and the other live steam—is no substitute.

"Seven minutes," said Bob. "If she's on time, we ought to hear her whistle right about now."

Bob has a sixth sense about the Nantucket steamers, of which he is a student. It didn't surprise me in the least when the whistle sounded, just as he finished his sentence.

"Captain Mims," said Bob with immense satisfaction, "always gives her a real good blast, doesn't he?"

"Real good," I commented. "Listen, Bob, do I *have* to go with you to meet the boat? Honestly, I'm about played out. I know it's your family and all that, but we saw them only a couple of weeks ago on the mainland, and we can drop in on them tomorrow."

"Whenever one of the family arrives on Nantucket," Bob informed me, still agreeably but with all the finality of a Supreme Court Justice handing down a unanimous opinion, "all the other members of the family who are here *always* meet the boat. You see, honey, it's *Tradition.*"

I remarked that if I had a nickel for each of the various exhausting activities which constituted Gilbreth Tradition at Nantucket we could afford to have a bathtub installed.

"Another way to get a bathtub," grinned Bob, "would be to charge admission to your sponge baths. If they're going to be semi-public anyway, we might as well cash in on them, eh?"

4

I realized that he knew how tired and depressed I was, and that he was only trying to get me into a better mood.

I realized he had worked just as hard as I, if not harder, during that first week of running Anchor Inn.

I realized that he had tried to get me a maid to help with the upstairs work, and that it was I who had declined for reasons of economy.

Even so, I did something that I don't do very often. I burst into tears. I simply couldn't help it.

"It's rough, isn't it honey?" Bob asked gently.

"But we're in Nantucket," I sobbed. "That's what you always wanted, isn't it?"

"I thought it was what you wanted, too," Bob whispered miserably.

I hate women who cry and I detest women who bawl, which was what I was doing. So I mopped my eyes on a nearby sheet and tried to keep things down to a muted bellow.

"I'm sorry, Bob," I choked. "Sure, I guess being in Nantucket is what I wanted, too."

"I'll bet," he continued, "you wish you were back on the mainland, don't you—back in our apartment with a regular salary check coming in every week! I don't blame you."

I thought of the apartment we had given up in New Jersey. It had been comfortable and fairly spacious, with privacy, closets, a separate bedroom for the baby, dressers, an all-electric kitchen and, yes, a six-foot bathtub. Up until a week ago, I had thought it a chore to make just one bed and Ann's crib.

"Don't be silly," I sniffed, still weeping a little in spite of everything I could do. "Are you all set? We'd better hurry. Did you remember about the lights?"

5

Bob rushed upstairs to turn on the lights in the halls. Meanwhile, I scribbled a note that, "Managers will be back at 8 p.m.," and thumbtacked it to the door. I felt guilty about leaving the inn even for the few minutes we'd be at the dock.

"Suppose," I asked Bob when he returned to the kitchen, "someone should phone with an important message for one of our guests."

"We'll have to take the chance—just this once," Bob said. "The operator would call back in twenty minutes, anyway."

He went over to the ice box, gingerly took out an egg, and placed it in a saucer on top. He didn't say anything, and he didn't have to. Miss Thomas, a prim spinster who had a single with a semi-private bath on the second floor, was particular about her morning egg. It had to be boiled exactly three minutes and it had to be at room temperature—rather than ice-box temperature—when it was immersed in boiling water. I don't know how she did it, but she could always tell when I forgot to take her egg out of the ice box the night before.

For some reason, the ridiculousness of her demands and her complaints restored my spirits. Bob slammed the ice-box door and glared at the lone egg on top, as if it symbolized all the problems and inconveniences and worries we had encountered during that past week.

"The old hag," he grumbled.

Bob brought Ann, basket and all, and we put her in the back seat of the car. She didn't wake up—our good little birthday girl. As we started for the dock, I could hear the fog horn at the end of the jetty, but the fog itself seemed to be lifting. If it were clear in the morning, Bob would be able to get the laundry dry.

"Just smell that wonderful Nantucket air, Barb," said Bob. "Doesn't it make you forget sponge baths and old battleaxes and

6

all the work at the inn? You know very well you wouldn't trade Nantucket for any place on the mainland!"

In retrospect, I can see I had ample warning of the way Bob felt about Nantucket. The first clue had come several years before, when he and I were planning our two-week wedding trip. Bob had said that of course we'd go to Nantucket. From his tone of voice, I gathered he took it for granted that no girl in her right mind would even consider going any place other than Nantucket for a wedding trip.

"Nantucket," I mentioned tentatively, "is that island off Cape Cod, isn't it?"

"Don't hand me that," Bob chuckled.

I didn't know it at the time, but it actually is inconceivable to him that everyone doesn't know all about Nantucket's location, history, vital statistics, topography, flora, fauna, boat schedules, annual rainfall and year-round mean temperature.

"And you'd rather go there than the Cape?" I asked, even more tentatively.

"Rather go to Nantucket than the Cape?" Bob laughed, and looked at me as if—what with my great sense of humor—our married life was going to be one big giggle. "That's rich, isn't it."

I decided I'd better go ahead and make a clean breast of it, before things got further out of hand.

"I've never," I blurted out, "been there."

Bob stopped laughing. "You've never been to Nantucket?" he asked. He couldn't have been much more patronizingly incredulous if I had just told him I had never learned the alphabet or never worn a pair of shoes. "You mean you were born in Massachusetts and brought up in Connecticut, only a few miles from Massachusetts, and you've never been on Nantucket?"

7

"Not once," I confessed, perhaps a little belligerently, because he was beginning to get under my skin. "Not only that, but I'm not even sure where it is. I *think* it's off Cape Cod."

"Good Lord," said Bob. And it wasn't an act; he simply couldn't believe it. "Born in Massachusetts, and she's never been to Nantucket."

"I guess I shouldn't have kept you in the dark about it," I snapped. "After all, I had no right leading you on, when I knew all the time the guilty secret I was harboring. Is the wedding off?"

But Bob wasn't listening. "Never been to Nantucket," he said, shaking his head. "Born in Massachusetts, and she's . . ."

"If we're going to be married," I replied with an attempt at dignity, "I'll thank you not to address me in the third person."

So, as I say, that was the first clue, and not a very subtle one. I should have realized right then that I was planning to marry a man who, in a sense, already was married—married to an island off Cape Cod, in Massachusetts; a moody tourist island, sometimes bright and beautiful and sometimes eerie and godforsaken.

Bob happens to come from a family of brothers and sisters who, besides being frighteningly numerous, are also tightly knit into an outspoken and dogmatic clan.

Bob sometimes admits this himself. As a matter of fact, when we told my mother about our engagement, he comforted her with:

"Don't think of it as losing a daughter, Mrs. Filer. Think of it as gaining a phalanx."

This phalanx can be counted upon to put up a solid front on certain basic matters, such as the desirability of Nantucket as the destination for a wedding trip.

In 1945, when Bob delivered to me the official pronouncement

8

of our honeymoon plans, I was aware of the numerical strength of the clan. But I was still in the dark about such important matters as Tradition. Consequently, I was naive enough to believe there was a possibility that the plans could be amended.

Not that I had anything against going to Nantucket. Still, I had a suspicion that, unless I made at least a show of asserting myself on this first decision, I would lose all the subsequent ones.

But the consensus, as I met future brother-in-law after future brother-in-law, not to mention future sister-in-law after future sister-in-law, seemed to be that I was almost as fortunate to be heading for Nantucket as I was to have captured the heart of the youngest Gilbreth brother. The fact that he was the only member of the family still unmarried, and the additional fact that as the eleventh in a sequence of a dozen children he had had unusual opportunities for indoctrination by the older members, were deemed to be the final proof of my hitting the matrimonial jackpot.

I don't mean to imply that they were all quite as wedded to the Island as Bob, who happened to be born there at the Gilbreths' summer house. But there wasn't much doubt that, given a free choice between the Garden of Eden and the Island of Nantucket, they would have voted for Nantucket to the last man.

"Of course," Bob told me a day or so later, "when we go to Nantucket we'll stay at The Shoe—that's Mother's summer cottage. I don't think any of the family will be there—or at least not very many."

"Aren't you afraid we'll be lonesome, off on a honeymoon all by ourselves with only a relatively small fraction of the family?" I couldn't resist asking.

"Don't worry," Bob assured me, "we'll probably never be home anyway. We'll be out clamming, fishing, and swimming. You won't need to pack a thing except a bathing suit, a couple of old shirts, and a pair of dungarees. You won't have to bother with any evening dresses or anything like that."

"That's a break for me, isn't it?" I said, thinking of the trousseau on which I had spent the accumulated savings of two years. "No dancing or eating out at fashionable restaurants or cocktails at the Yacht Club or any boring stuff like that."

"You said it," Bob agreed enthusiastically. "That sort of stuff is for the *summer* people."

"And you're not summer people?"

"We go there only in the summers, yes," he explained patiently. "But we certainly are not summer people. Remember, I was *born* there."

Remember it? As if I would ever be allowed to forget it!

Nantucket or not and big family or not, I knew that Bob was— as the cliché goes—the man for me. Also, it is only fair to say that he is a reasonable, undictatorial citizen on subjects which do not pertain to that island. However, I wasn't going to surrender entirely on the matter of having no voice in planning my own wedding trip.

We finally effected what I thought to be somewhat of a compromise, however one-sided: We'd spend three days on Cape Cod, which I had always liked, and the balance of the time on Nantucket.

We each had vacations of two weeks—Bob from a personnel job with a large electrical corporation in New York and I from a chemical research job with an aviation company in New Jersey. We had both recently finished college. Since neither of us had yet been made a junior partner in his company, I couldn't put up a very strong argument against using the Gilbreths' summer cottage. I did hope, though, that not more than a fourth of his family

—which is to say three of his brothers or sisters, three of his in-laws, and nine or ten of his nieces and nephews—would be on hand.

We were married in late August, and spent the first night of our wedding trip at the Publick House in Sturbridge, Massachusetts. The next morning was warm and clear, and Bob was up with the sun, packing his bag.

"Good morning, darling," I greeted him. "How does it feel to wake up in the morning and find that you have a wife?"

"Great," Bob beamed. "Marvelous. And look at the day—isn't the weather perfect?"

"Divine," I agreed.

"I'll bet," said Bob, "the weather on Nantucket is perfect today, too."

Well, there was Nantucket elbowing her way into the conversation again. I thought, though, that perhaps I had scored a moral victory by getting him to admit by implication that sometimes the weather wasn't perfect.

We went down to breakfast, and Bob disappeared to make a phone call. When he returned fifteen minutes later, he was much too excited to eat.

"I've checked with the Weather Bureau," he said. "It's clear as a bell at Nantucket."

"That takes a big load off my mind," I told him, suspecting that the battle had been lost.

"Sometimes, you know," he continued in the first of the many informative lectures I was to receive on meteorology as applied to Nantucket, "it can be clear in all of Massachusetts, but foggy on Nantucket. On the other hand, sometimes it can be clear in Nantucket and dismal over all the rest of Massachusetts."

"Amazing," I said as icily as I knew how. But Bob was too wrapped up in Nantucket to notice.

"Isn't it? I made another call, too—to the steamship office in Woods Hole. They say they'll squeeze the car on the boat this afternoon, if you want to change our plans and go to Nantucket today."

"But how about our hotel reservations on the Cape?" I asked. And by now I was sure the battle was lost.

"I knew how you'd feel," Bob grinned, "so I made a couple of other phone calls and cancelled them. Okay?"

I've always believed that when you can't beat them, you join them. "Okay, swell," I said, and I tried to sound sincere. "How many of your family will be there, I wonder?"

"I'm sorry, Barb, but not a one," replied Bob, apologizing for this thoughtless desertion of his kin in our hour of need. "But never you mind. I think just the two of us will be able to manage the sailboat all right, provided you can give me a hand with the jib."

I promised that whatever the jib was, I'd give a hand.

Bob paid the bill for our breakfast, after doing a double-take at the size of the check. I think it was the breakfast bill that brought home the realization that he was now paying for two—and would be for the rest of his life, except when he was paying for three or four.

While he restlessly paced the bedroom, I packed so hastily that I forgot my negligee, my best shoes and the only hat I had brought with me. But that turned out to be all right. We eventually picked them up two weeks later and, as Bob had pointed out, we didn't need anything much at Nantucket except dungarees, old shirts and bathing suits.

We boarded the steamer at Woods Hole, Massachusetts, in a terrifying maneuver which involved driving our Ford up a flimsy-looking gangplank only a few inches wider than the car fenders. While thanking the Lord that we didn't own a Cadillac, I also took the precaution of cranking down the windows to give us a fighting chance of escape, in case Bob misjudged his distances.

"Why I could do this with my eyes closed," he assured me, and that happened to be exactly the way his passenger *was* doing it. "I know every inch of these Nantucket steamers. After all, I've been riding them every summer since I can remember."

You see, he was born there!

When I finally opened my eyes, I found we were deep in the dark bowels of the vessel.

"Back her up five feet, Bawbby boy," an ancient seagoing flunky was instructing him, "and then pull her into the lane by the port bulkhead. You know where to put her."

"Aye-aye, Al," Bob replied as smugly as if the Prince of Wales had just done him the honor of remembering his name.

"Now leave her in gear, leave the keys in the ignition and don't lock the doors," commanded the flunky.

"Aye-aye, Al," said Bob.

We climbed out of the car and went upstairs—or topside, if you insist, and Bob does—and found seats on the top deck near the back. The weather was still beautiful—not just beautiful, gorgeous. The water was purple blue, with just a few whitecaps outside the harbor. If you know that part of the country, you'll know how invigorating the air felt and how wonderful it smelled. I was beginning to think that Bob had been right in cancelling our hotel reservations and pushing up our departure for Nantucket. I stretched out in my deck chair. The sun was warm and good.

Maybe I was just a silly, romantic girl, but after all I had been married only twenty-four hours. At any rate, I reached out and took Bob's hand.

Bob was sitting up straight in his chair, following intently every move by the men on the dock.

13

"Now," he told me, "I'll have the lines singled up, and then I'll have one long blast on the whistle. Look alive there."

The men on the dock, as if they had heard him, cast off one of each double rope which held the steamer to the pier. As they did so, the whistle gave one long and very loud blast which, since Bob liked the whistle and had chosen seats by it, almost blasted me out of my deck chair.

"Cast off," Bob commanded, again to me but precisely as if he were giving the orders.

The men cast off.

"Now I'll have two short blasts on the whistle, and I want you to hug that black buoy as we leave the harbor."

"Do we have to have two blasts on the whistle?" I pouted.

"Yes," Bob replied sternly. "Right now."

The whistle gave two short blasts, and we practically took the barnacles off the black buoy as Woods Hole began to disappear.

"You think you're pretty smart, don't you?" I teased him, and Bob finally discovered he was holding my hand—or at any rate that I was holding his.

"It's going to be a wonderful honeymoon," he grinned. "You're not sorry about anything, are you?"

I told him I wasn't sorry about anything.

"And wait," he said, "until you see the *Cross Rip* lightship. That's after Oak Bluffs, which is at Martha's Vineyard, of course."

"Does the ferry stop at Oak Bluffs?" I asked.

Bob looked self-consciously around. Then he leaned over and put his head up close to mine. That was more like it, I thought. Up there on the top deck, with the seagulls circling off the stern and the wake leaving a white river across the ocean, was certainly a romantic spot, all right. I figured it had to be, to get Bob's mind even momentarily away from Nantucket.

14

"Barb, honey," he whispered, "I should have told you about this before. I know it's my fault, and I don't want you to think I'm blaming you for it. But please, never, never again call this steamer a 'ferry.' There is nothing that irritates a Nantucketer more than to call his steamer a ferry. Will you try to remember that?"

"Aye, aye, Al," I told him.

For much of the remainder of the journey, I got a play-by-play account of some of Bob's previous crossings to Nantucket.

It developed that the steamer on which we were cruising was a far cry indeed from the *Uncatena,* a side-wheeler, which was the first Nantucket boat that Bob remembered. Next after the *Uncatena* came a sea-going arrow called the *Gay Head,* which had a walking beam on the top deck and side paddlewheels. Next was the *Sankaty,* the first of the Nantucket boats with propellers. Then came the steamers *Naushon, Nantucket, New Bedford,* and *Martha's Vineyard.*

All were good-sized vessels, capable of carrying nine hundred to one thousand passengers and seaworthy enough to cross the Atlantic and keep right on going around the world, Bob told me as proudly as if he had personally laid the keel of each of them.

On those earlier Nantucket steamers, there sometimes would be seven or eight of the Gilbreth youngsters on board, under the charge of an older sister who had all the disciplinary powers of the senior officer present. They'd still manage to elude her and sneak up onto the bridge or down into the engine room. They were not exactly welcome in either place, since both were forbidden to passengers. However, the succession of captains and crews eventually came to realize that the Gilbreth children outnumbered the men who could be spared from their duties to chase them away.

Finally, the tribe was usually tolerated on the bridge, provided the Indians did not try to blow the whistle, touch the wheel, operate the engine telegraph, or give the captain the word about the tricky Woods Hole and Nantucket channels. And they were tolerated in the engine room, provided they left the shoveling of coal to the men who had been specifically hired for that fascinating privilege, and provided they kept reasonably clear of the moving machinery.

In fact there was one skipper, Captain Durfee, who—rather than having them sneak through his legs, hide under his bunk, and sometimes borrow his binoculars—would order chairs brought up on the bridge and would sit Bob and some of his brothers down, where he could keep a weather eye on them.

Naturally, Bob got to know every landmark and every buoy on the four-hour steamer trip. He even learned the navigational idiosyncrasies of the various captains: When each would make his turn as he passed a marker, and when and where each would order the whistle blown—and how many times.

As we approached the *Cross Rip* lightship, which is about halfway between Oak Bluffs and Nantucket, Bob also gave me the history of some of the earlier lightships with that same name—a name, incidentally, which I had associated previously only with saws.

The weather was still beautiful, but the ocean was a little rough. I was beginning to feel slightly seasick. I didn't know then as much about Nantucket Tradition as I know now. I had an idea, nevertheless, that getting seasick might be considered an even worse breach of etiquette than calling the steamer a ferry. Fortunately, the seasick feeling did not last long, and I proved to be an acceptable sailor.

The reader will doubtless be as interested as I was to learn that the *Cross Rip* marks treacherous tides and shoals. The experiences of previous lightships at anchor there would make a book in themselves. The anchor lines have parted and ships have wallowed helplessly. Men have been lost overboard in the raging seas. One *Cross Rip,* caught in an ice floe, went out to sea with all hands, and never was heard from again. Not to this very day!

Bob explained that, when he was a youngster, the steamer would pass as close as she safely could to the lightship, and that passengers would throw newspapers and magazines to the *Cross Rip* crew. I gathered that you could tell the experienced Nantucket travelers from the neophytes, in those days, because the experienced ones would start wrapping their periodicals, for throwing purposes, shortly after the steamer left Oak Bluffs.

To have a tightly tied newspaper, when the steamer approached the *Cross Rip,* was considered a mark of *savoir faire*. Needless to say, Bob used to start acquiring newspapers even before boarding the steamer. By the time he had reached the lightship, he usually had enough wrapped newspapers to deliver a whole route, and there was a serious drought of reading material for the remainder of the passage.

Because of radio news and better mail service, the steamers had abandoned—some years before our honeymoon—the practice of passing close enough to the lightship for newspaper hurling. It was plain that Bob thought this to be a great pity.

The first landfall as you approach Nantucket is a plain black, cylindrical water tank. As I found out later, it is situated on the north bluff, about halfway between the jetties and the small settlement of Madaket.

Bob started looking for it as soon as we passed the *Cross Rip,* and I got the idea there must be something quite special about it. Pacing the starboard bow on the top deck, he located the tower within a matter of minutes. Then he became increasingly annoyed because—no matter how steadily he pointed and no matter how steadily I sighted along his outstretched arm—I couldn't immediately spot it.

Meanwhile, quite a few passengers who had been noticing Bob's excited gestures came to the rail and started shading their eyes and looking, too. I don't believe any of them had the least idea what they were looking *for*. I suppose that if a sperm whale had breached close aboard and three points off the starboard beam, they wouldn't have been any more surprised than to learn that the mere sight of a water tower had caused one of the passengers to throw what my Grandma Filer would describe as a conniption fit.

About ten minutes later, I too could make out the water tower, standing like a shadowy needle in the haze of the atmosphere.

"I see the water tower," I whispered, because I didn't want the other passengers to know what had caused all the commotion. "The water tower is right there." I pointed myself, and Bob nodded in approval. I did not add that in my home town of Somers, Connecticut, we had silos that were just as big, if not bigger, and almost identically shaped—and that no one ever got the least bit excited about any of them when they loomed up on the horizon.

But the view of the town of Nantucket, as you enter the narrow channel at the end of the jetties, is something very special. Bob hadn't exaggerated its beauty. In the foreground, of course, was the ocean—calm now and purple blue. Behind the perimeter of sparkling, yellow beach were the green of well-tended yards and the darker green of wild rose bushes growing in meadows. The sun was just setting, and the weathered shingles of the old houses gleamed like polished silver. A flash of gold came from the gilded dome of the handsome Old South Church.

Sitting back beyond the meadows was a rolling cliff. Its almost vertical face, planted in grass, formed the front yards of hotel-sized, two and three-story "cottages" of wealthy summer residents.

Actually, they were mansions, but if it was the local custom to refer to them modestly as cottages, I was perfectly willing to do as the Romans.

"I can see The Shoe now," Bob all but shouted in excitement. "There's our cottage over there."

I never have been any good at looking along a person's arm to find the specific object at which he is pointing—as witness my trouble in locating the water tower. The job is all the more impossible when the owner of the arm is standing on the deck of a moving boat and having difficulty in restraining himself from jumping over the rail and swimming ashore.

This time, when I looked along Bob's arm, I thought he was indicating one of the mansions on The Cliff.

He certainly was pointing in that direction.

I had to concede mentally that, just as Bob hadn't exaggerated Nantucket's beauty, neither had he nor my in-laws exaggerated the charm of their summer cottage.

"Now I'll have three short blasts on the whistle," Bob ordered— and I covered my ears just in time. "Mind," he added, "that you hug Brant Point as you come into the inner harbor. Look alive, now."

2 ~ Pennies for Heaven

The drive from the steamer toward The Shoe further confirmed everything Bob had said about Nantucket. I could see that the island was somewhat like Cape Cod, only minus the tourist cabins, clam bars, Howard Johnsons and Ye Auld Pirates Roostes.

We took a short detour past the Dreamland Theater and the Atheneum Library so that we could ride down the two wide blocks of Main Street, the island's business center. Main Street hasn't been changed very much since it was laid out before the Revolution. Sensibly, Nantucketers never got around to modernizing it, when the rest of the country was improving things by sawing down shade trees, laying tracks for trolleys, removing benches from in front of stores, and replacing horse troughs with traffic signals.

Main Street is wide enough so that automobiles can park nose-first at both curbs, and still leave plenty of room for traffic. It is paved with the cobblestones which whaling schooners brought back as ballast after delivering cargoes of sperm oil. Old wine-glass elms tower above the stores and almost join branches over the street.

The stores were crowded with summer residents, most of whom displayed healthy-looking tans, and there was a queue running into Roger's, to pick up newspapers which had arrived on our steamer.

As we headed toward The Shoe, I noticed that Nantucketers also had resisted the trend toward Victorian architecture, which came along at about the same time the shade trees began to disappear from our cities. Almost all of the houses in the village are Colonial, although Colonial simplicity sometimes became severity, at the hands of the frivolity-hating Quakers who built many of the original homes. Some of the old houses, crowded close together for company, have railed balconies on their roofs. These, as even I knew, are the widow-walks—so called because many a Nantucket woman of a hundred and fifty or more years ago scanned the horizon with a telescope from the lofty platforms, for a ship that might never return.

After leaving the village, I experienced for the first time the spicy smell of bayberry bushes in the meadows—a scent which I cannot precisely describe, but which is tangy, clean and utterly delicious—and which I will always associate with Nantucket.

I also observed, as we drove along in the twilight, that we were headed not for The Cliff, with its summer mansions, but for the low-lying area at the foot of The Cliff. When Bob stopped the car in front of The Shoe, I thought at first there must surely be some mistake.

I don't want to give the impression that Bob or his brothers and sisters had ever so much as intimated to me that their cottage at

Nantucket was any more than a cottage. After all, I was the one who had made the error in locating The Shoe, when I looked along Bob's arm from the deck of the steamer. I also realize now that their enthusiasm for the cottage was based on nostalgia, rather than physical beauty or convenience.

Be that as it may, I was unprepared for The Shoe. I would have been unprepared, even if I hadn't made the mistake of thinking it was on The Cliff. So would anybody.

In the first place, it was flanked by two lighthouses, which were a part of the property. They were built more than a hundred years ago and sold, probably fifty-odd years ago, by the government as surplus property.

The lighthouses, I discovered, were now used as extra bedrooms when the Gilbreth clan converged en masse on Nantucket. Despite their age, they were in splendid repair when contrasted with the cottage itself. The Shoe originally had been the lightkeeper's tool house, and I think was sort of thrown in as something to boot when the government sold the lighthouses. Although a couple of wings had been added to the tool house, it still resembled—more than anything else—a tool house. As tool houses go, it was neither especially quaint nor substantial. Even if I had been a carpenter looking desperately for a place to store my implements, I don't think I would have taken The Shoe as a present.

The shifting sands had caused the walls to sag and the roof to billow. Of course, as I found out the first time we had a heavy dew, the roof also leaked. Some of the windows bore wooden triangles at their tops to compensate for spaces created by tilting timbers. Even so, the windows didn't fit their frames very well. The foundations were beginning to rot, and signs of corrective amateur carpentry—performed earlier that summer by Bob's older brothers—were apparent on all sides.

23

"Isn't it *something?*" Bob asked me proudly.

It was something, all right, but he wasn't going to trap me into saying what.

Although any burglar could have entered the place by pulling a couple of planks off the wall and climbing in, the front door was secured by two large padlocks, which Bob proceeded to open. Once inside, Bob led me from room to room pointing out conveniences and obvious advantages.

"In case you want to learn the Morse Code, for instance," he shouted from the bathroom, "come in here and look."

I had no intention of spending a honeymoon learning the Morse Code, but I went in and looked. The code was painted on the bathroom wall, where Bob's father had stenciled it twenty-five years before, so that his children could memorize it during intervals of what Mr. Gilbreth—a motion-study expert—termed "unavoidable delay."

In case I wanted to know whether Jupiter was a larger planet than Venus, I could study the interesting drawings which Mr. Gilbreth had made on the whitewashed walls in the dining room.

In case I wanted to see whether I was taller now than Bob was at the age of fourteen, I could measure myself in a doorway which contained marks showing the heights of Bob and all my in-laws, from the year they were old enough to walk until the year they finally got their growth.

Since all of the codes, drawings, and markings were Tradition, no one had wanted to paint or whitewash over them. The ancient whitewash had long since started to flake off. The result was not particularly handsome, and any violent movement would provoke a miniature snowstorm.

I digress here long enough to relate that when the wife of one of

Bob's brothers came to Nantucket for the first time, she made the mistake of applying a coat of paint to a particularly disreputable-looking rocking chair, in the bedroom to which she was assigned. The rocking chair, by no stretch of the imagination, could be described as an antique. And there was not the slightest disagreement that it sorely needed a coat of paint. But the rocking chair happened to be Tradition. After spending two summers in Coventry, she finally got some paint remover and sandpaper, and restored the monstrosity to its original gruesomeness. This seemed to satisfy everyone, and she was widely commended for being such a good sport about the matter.

I noticed, among other things, as Bob led me through the house skillfully groping for and finding light fixtures in the most unlikely places, that while the bathroom was equipped with the Morse Code, it was not equipped with bath, shower, or hot water. It turned out that there was a cold shower in the basement, though. Also, whatever cooking I did would have to be on a coal stove. I didn't know it at the time, but my honeymoon was to prove excellent training for my subsequent career as co-owner and chambermaid of Anchor Inn.

In the days that followed, we did everything that was Tradition and still found time for a few things that perhaps were not.

One of Bob's favorite pastimes is quahauging and little necking (a pun may seem called for, but I think it best to resist it) "out Polpis way." I can't be more specific than that about the location, because it is classified within the family as top secret.

Nantucketers are reluctant to disclose, even to each other, the whereabouts of their favorite places to dig clams, catch fish, and gather blueberries and beach plums. Ask a boy selling blueberries where he picked them, and he'll usually point vaguely in a quarter circle and reply "out Quidnet way" or "out Surfside way." Try to pin him down, and he may tell you, "I more than likely couldn't find the place again myself."

So it had been a stroke of pure luck when Bob's oldest sister, Anne, had discovered the quahaug and little neck bed, years before. Anne had steered their sailboat into a cove to fix the rudder, had jumped over the side in neck-deep water, and had felt a quahaug with her bare feet. Further exploration located a little neck bed in closer to shore.

Bob stressed the secrecy so often, before we went clamming, that I wouldn't have been too surprised if he had taken me there blindfolded.

As we drove in bathing suits on the Wauwinet Road "out Polpis way," Bob kept glancing furtively in the rear-view mirror. And before he turned off the Wauwinet Road on a certain dirt road, he pulled our car over on the shoulder and parked until he was satisfied we hadn't been followed.

"How in the world would anyone know we were headed for a secret clam bed?" I inquired.

"Some of the people up on The Cliff might have seen me put the buckets in the car," Bob explained. "They'd probably give their eye teeth to know where we get our little necks. And next year, the bed would be empty."

When we got out of the car at the end of the dirt road, we had to walk a fairly long distance in a certain direction along a boggy beach, to reach the shore line adjacent to the clam bed. I noticed for the first time that while Bob had optimistically brought two buckets, he had neglected to bring clam rakes. When I asked him about it, he explained:

"That would be a *dead* giveaway. Besides, that's not the best way to get the good-sized little necks we're going after."

It developed that the good-sized little necks were in waist deep water, and buried two or three inches under a rocky, shell-filled, evil-smelling black ooze. To get them, you crouched down until the water was up to your neck, and dug with your fingers into the mud. The crouching, although quite tiring, left only a relatively small target above the water for vicious green flies which inhabit that boggy part of the shoreline.

At first I brought up more stones than little necks, and broke my fingernails in the process. But I finally got the hang of it. When I learned what the hinge of a buried little neck feels like, I could even locate them with my feet, as Bob was doing. Then I cut my right foot on a shell.

The buckets, meanwhile, had been filled with water and placed on the bottom. Bob had fastened a string and a small wooden float to each handle, so that we could find them in the black mud we were stirring.

It took about an hour of actual digging to fill the buckets. Our total time in the water was about three hours, though, because we had to quit every time a sailboat approached, and pretend that we were swimming. Bob did handstands, porpoise dives and other aquatic gyrations designed to give the impression that we were merely frolicking in the bay. However, since the island abounds with fly-free, beautiful, sandy beaches, anyone who thought we were really swimming in that smelly slime must also have thought we were crazy.

At the end of the three hours, I was blue with cold and my skin was water soaked into corrugations. I limped back to the car on my cut foot, opened the trunk, and gave the signal that the coast was clear on the land side. After making certain that the coast was also clear of sailboats, Bob raced up with the full buckets, shoved them into the trunk, slammed the trunk closed, and then breathed a sigh of relief.

"That's always the risky part of the deal," he said.

I don't know what we would have done if someone had come down the dirt road toward our car, while Bob was making the final dash with the clam-filled buckets. I suppose we would have had to eliminate the intruder.

The little necks, which I've never liked but which I ate that night so as not to disappoint Bob, made me sick to my stomach.

Subsequently, we fished with drop lines off the jetties, we fished with surf-casting rods off Smith's Point, and we fished with trolling lines from the family sailboat. I accidentally stuck a fishhook in my elbow and got blisters on my hands from handling the jib.

We went swimming in the smooth waters of the harbor and in the rough waters of the South Shore. Bob tried to teach me how to get boiled in the surf. I tried it once and pulled up lame, with two inches sanded off my left knee.

I had tetanus shots for my cut foot and fishhook-punctured elbow.

I wrestled with the coal stove, froze in the cold shower, put unguents on a second-degree sunburn, and was kept awake nights by the indescribably mournful moaning of the jetty foghorn.

One night we drove out to Sankaty Lighthouse, on a high, sheer bluff near Siasconset. The phosphorescent surf counted a rumbling cadence from below, and a wind so strong that it tugged at my hair and skirt blew the tangy bayberry scent from the moors. I looked up at the eight dazzling rays of light, sending segments out into the sea, and realized they were warning away from shoals ships as far as thirty miles distant from Nantucket. For a moment it seemed that Bob and I were alone on a promontory in the middle of the ocean, with the light doing sentry duty to keep out unwanted visitors.

Pennies for Heaven

We walked the mellowed old brick sidewalks of the village, past the quaint houses and the brick mansions built with sperm-oil money; past the Pacific National Bank, so named because the capital used to establish it came from whales caught in the Pacific; past the Maria Mitchell Observatory, named for the first woman in the world to discover a comet—a discovery, incidentally, made from the roof of the bank.

We ate at a lamp-lit restaurant where broiled lobster, prepared by Danish cooks, was served in the surroundings of Nantucket antiques, early Colonial implements, and the coppery glow of old pine planks.

We explored the wharves and the inner harbor, where two hundred sailing ships at a time had once taken on supplies to search the seas in the hope of finding greasy luck—a fortune in oil. There still were many signs of the days when Nantucket was the whaling hub of the world; when Nantucket ships provided the oil, whale bone and ambergris to light the lamps, lace the ladies and scent the perfume in half the capitals of the globe.

One cool day we walked the moors through heather, mealy plum, and low-bush blueberries to the site of Sherburne, the first white settlement on the island.

We visited the Kenneth Taylor Art Gallery, in an old warehouse with beams so large a man can scarcely circle them with his arms; the Old Mill, where the early settlers ground their maize into cornmeal; and the Whaling Museum.

The Whaling Museum fascinated me. When I said I'd like to know more about whaling, Bob took me to call on a year-round lady resident who knows a good bit about it. A dainty spinster, no longer young, and a particular friend of Bob's family, she served us tea and told me that her lovely crocheted doilies came from her "hopeless chest."

29

Most of her stories had to do with cannibalism, and I've since verified some of them at the library. She told them with considerable relish, while nibbling fastidiously on the refreshments which she offered: Olive sandwiches and—appropriately, I thought —lady fingers.

It's quite true that cannibalism is a minor but dramatic part of Nantucket's whaling history. It should be remembered that casualties were heavy among the whaling schooners, which sailed around Cape Horn into uncharted waters of the North and South Pacific. It was not at all unusual for crews from wrecked vessels to sail a thousand miles in open dories. Sometimes the shipwrecked mariners landed on South Sea Islands, and were eaten by cannibals. Sometimes they were accepted by the cannibals, took native wives, and themselves became devotees of the practice of eating human flesh.

Cannibalism was not unheard of, either, among whaling crews starving in the open dories. There is one documented case wherein the shipwrecked men aboard a dory commanded by a Captain Pollard drew lots to see whom they would eat. Fate selected Captain Pollard's nephew, Owen Coffin, as the man who came to be the dinner. The diners did ample justice to Owen. Ironically, a short time after the feast was concluded and the groaning board cleared, Captain Pollard and his crew were rescued by another Nantucket whaler.

When Pollard got back to Nantucket, he must have had an embarrassing job in breaking the news to his and Owen's joint kin. Pollard wasn't entirely ostracized, and in fact went back to sea as the master of several other vessels. But he always had trouble signing on new crew members. Especially fat ones, I guess. Bad luck dogged him, too, and he eventually was grounded—or made to "swallow the anchor," as the expression went in those days.

Pennies for Heaven

The story of poor Owen Coffin recalls another and more recent tale, which may or may not be true but which I have subsequently heard told and retold on Nantucket.

It seems that, about fifty years ago, a reporter from a Boston paper made a special trip to Nantucket to get an interview with a former whaling master who was celebrating his ninetieth birthday. In the course of the interview, the reporter disclosed that he himself had descended on his mother's side from Nantucket whaling men.

"Perhaps," said the reporter, "you might have known my great grandfather, sir. His name was William Folger. We understand that he died in a dory in the North Pacific."

"Know him," cackled the old man. "Know him? Why, boy, I *et* him."

When Bob and I were roaming the wharves, we also ran into the present-day equivalent of the old Nantucket whaling stories. We had stopped to pass the time of day with a gay and ancient old reprobate who sometimes rents out his catboat and whose breath suggested that sunshine was not entirely responsible for his florid complexion.

"Any news, Cap'n?" asked Bob, who liked to award that title to all male Nantucketers over the age of thirty-five who owned as much as an oarlock in the way of sea going equipment.

"Not much, boy," replied the cap'n. "Been little news around the waterfront since last week when that Vineyarder was towed in by the Coast Guard. Never was a Vineyarder who was more than a tack and a reach from being an idiot, when you put him in a boat."

"Landlubbers?" I asked.

"This one," he chuckled, "had a hankering to go to Hyannis in his cruiser. He started out and his motor quit. Then a fog come

31

up. Drifted out to sea and didn't know where he was at. He had a fishhook and a piece of string aboard, but no bait. Third day out, he commenced to get hungry, and thought he was starving to death. You know what he done?"

I waited patiently for the denouement, but the cap'n was so convulsed at recalling the plight of the Martha's Vineyard native that he had difficulty continuing.

"I'll tell you what he done," he finally managed. "He cut off one of his little toes and put it on the fishhook. Love a duck. Ho-he-ho."

Shaking with merriment, the cap'n started to walk away. "Ho-he-ho."

"No kidding?" I called after him.

He turned around, purple from guffawing, and held up his hands, palms first, as if to indicate that he had better stop thinking about the story before he perished of mirth.

"But what happened?" I insisted. "Did he catch anything with his little toe?"

With a great deal of effort, the cap'n finally got enough breath to blurt out in an exhaling explosion: "Fish stole his bait. Ho-he-ho. Ho-ho."

Then the cap'n hurried away, still shaking, and waving a hand behind his back to signify that, if we had a humane bone in our bodies, we wouldn't press him further.

I don't want to sound like the conclusion of a travelogue, but the sun *was* high in its zenith as Bob and I finally boarded the steamer to leave beautiful Nantucket, the Little Grey Lady of the Sea. Not only could I see the sun, I also could hear the booming but decorous tones of the old Portuguese bell in the town clock tower, chiming fifty-two times, which it does every day at high noon; as well as at the 9 p.m. curfew and at 7 a.m., when all decent people are supposed to be off the streets and up and about, respectively.

This time, Bob so hated to leave that he couldn't put much heart into his "commands" about singling up the lines and taking in the gangplanks.

"Did you like it, honey?" he asked me. "What do you *really* think of Nantucket?"

"I don't know," I said, quite truthfully because I hadn't quite made up my mind then. As a matter of fact, it was a question I was turning over, even as he asked it.

"If you didn't like it," volunteered Bob in what was certainly the supreme sacrifice, "we can go someplace else next summer."

The steamer started to edge away from the dock.

"I hope I didn't run you ragged, with the fishing, clamming, sailing and all," Bob apologized. "It's just that when you've only got two weeks there's not much time to crowd in everything you've been looking forward to for a whole year. I guess there's not much doubt that I'm off my rocker when it comes to Nantucket."

I said that was all right—that I understood.

"I'm not going to bore you on the way home with any more monologs about the island," he promised. "But there's just one more thing that's Tradition. When the steamer rounds Brant Point, there's a superstition that those who throw a penny overboard will always return to Nantucket. I could mention that the second lighthouse in the whole United States was built on Brant Point—but that's one of the things I'm not going to bore you with."

The wharves and the village built with sperm oil money were falling astern, and something was happening to my swallowing apparatus that answered the question I had been turning over in my mind.

33

Bob was watching me out of the corner of his eye as we came abreast of Brant Point. The upper deck was crowded with returning vacationers, but when I tossed a coin over the rail, Bob pushed three men aside so that he would have ample elbow room to kiss the bride.

3 ~ Bathrooms Are Bread and Butter

I had the Nantucket bug bad—so bad that it was I, rather than Bob, who suggested we save our money and make a down-payment on an inn there. We lived in the small apartment in Bloomfield, New Jersey, and got along on Bob's salary while banking most of mine. He commuted to his personnel job in New York and I commuted to my chemical research job in Caldwell, New Jersey.

We didn't see much of each other, and neither of us liked that. It was the usual, frantic hello-dear-and-goodbye routine of today's suburban gladiators. Hail and farewell.

No use to go into it here. Hail and don't forget to set the alarm. Farewell and if you run you can still make the seven:forty-seven.

The process of saving took three years. But by the end of the second year, Ann was bought and paid for and we still had enough money so that—with what we borrowed—we could start looking for the inn.

Consequently, two summers after our wedding trip, we were back on the steamer again, headed for Nantucket. It was early September, with the vacation season drawing to a close. Ann was three months old, and we had left her with my folks while we went inn-hunting.

During the two-year interval, we had read books on accounting, plumbing, carpentering, restoring old furniture, and what to look for when you are buying a house. We had listened to lengthy if well-meaning advice from the members of Bob's family and my own. Bob's family seemed fairly well agreed that we should look before we leaped. My family, coming from New England, had definite ideas about spending money which boiled down to the basic belief that one usually shouldn't.

But more valuable than the books we had read and the family advice was an off-the-cuff warning we received on the steamer that September, from a fellow passenger.

He was a retired textile man, plump and astute, who had been going to Nantucket even longer than Bob's family. Bob knew him, of course, and we got to talking. When Bob asked him what he thought about our plan to buy an inn, he advised:

"In the first place, don't. In the second place, when you *do,* remember that bathrooms are bread and butter. I've stayed in inns all over the country. I know what I'm talking about."

"But it's got to be an old Colonial place, too, doesn't it?" Bob inquired.

"An inn on Nantucket should be quaint, yes. The summer visitors expect that. But count the bathrooms first—even before you measure the width of the floorboards for quaintness or examine the roofs for leaks."

"How about location?" I put in.

"You'll want to be in the village, since most of your guests won't have cars. But bathrooms are more important. Before you buy, start at each bedroom and see how far you have to walk to get to a bath. Do you see what I mean, Bobby?"

Bob and I both answered affirmatively, since "Bobby" is a nickname we both wear—although with reluctance. I prefer Barb and he prefers Bob, and we both resist the collective nickname of The Bobbies, which some of Bob's brothers attempted to pin on us when we started talking about buying an inn. Because of our one-track minds on the subject, we had become "The Bobby Twins on Nantucket Isle," "The Bobby Twins in the Tourist Trade," and other variations of the same theme. After the humor of the theme had been exhausted—in fact, *long* after—the titles were shortened to The Bobbies.

On reaching Nantucket, we stayed again at The Shoe, while looking at inns and old houses which might be converted into inns. There is never a big turnover of real estate within the town of Nantucket, because many islanders have been brought up in the belief that Nantucket property is the soundest of long-range, conservative investments. Let depressions come and go, let the mainland indulge in wild speculations and slumps—a Nantucketer who has property on the island will never starve.

This urge to hold onto island real estate extends even to non-revenue-producing property. For instance, we had noticed an empty lot which was ideally located, and had toyed with the idea of building a new inn, in reproduction Colonial. After some searching through records at the Town Building—whose old bricks, incidentally, look as if they had been laid by someone who had just stepped off a rolling ship—we found the name of the owner and I telephoned her.

37

"Not for sale," she told me.

More out of curiosity than from any belief that she would change her mind, I asked:

"Do you mind telling me what you plan to do with it?"

"*Keep* it," she replied.

A few inns, however, were listed for sale. The candid opinion of the realtors with whom we made contact was that each inn was a gold mine which would soon put us on easy street. Since one of the thoroughfares on Nantucket actually is named Easy Street, the realtors had a good out if anyone tried to pin them down.

Bob, who is less inhibited about such matters than I, made every attempt to pin them. Bob wanted to know why, if an inn was a gold mine, the mineowners were not content to continue the extraction of nuggets from their diggings.

This inquiry evoked two different types of implications from the realtors. One was that there had been a death, and it was necessary to dispose of the property at a give-away price in order to settle an estate. The other was that the owner had reaped such a fortune from his gold mine that he intended to retire and presumably to live a luxurious life at various European spas.

New England realtors, in general, have all the instincts of their horse-trading forebears. Superimposed on these instincts is a sound knowledge of modern psychology. The irresistible combination of the old instincts and the new knowledge is one of the reasons that hundreds of New Yorkers have fallen all over each other to pay minor fortunes for cranberry bogs and fishing shacks along the whole length of Cape Cod.

Of New England realtors, the Nantucket species is the most—as the islanders would put it—"some" sharp. "Some," on Nantucket, is a superlative approximately equivalent to super colossally, and is part of the Nantucketer's tendency toward cautious understatement. The exception to this rule of understatement is the realtor himself.

The asking prices, in some cases, were twice what the owners would settle for, if they had to. This practice of double-pricing, leaving plenty of margin for reductions in the face-to-face bargaining sessions, actually serves to create good will all around.

For instance, when a double-priced summer house is finally sold for only fifty per cent more than what it is worth, the seller naturally is pleased. As for the off-island buyer, he will go through the rest of his life in the pleasant belief that his city-slicker methods of haggling—sometimes including the waving of large sums of currency under the realtor's nose, to clinch a quick cash sale at a "reduced" price—have resulted in buncoing the natives.

But some of the real estate men got off on the wrong foot with Bob by treating us as summer people.

"When you've been around Nantucket as long as I have," one realtor told us patronizingly, "you will realize the charm of the island and why most people are so reluctant to part with their homes!"

"How long have you been around Nantucket?" asked Bob.

"I'm practically a native," the realtor smiled. "I moved here ten years ago."

"I," glared Bob, *"am* a native."

Neither the fact that Bob happened to be born on Nantucket nor the additional fact that he also happened to be born on Nantucket on Independence Day had any immediate effect on asking prices of houses. But we did have four price-lowering arguments that neither horse-trading nor psychology could turn aside. If we bought an inn at all, it had to have enough rooms to yield us a subsistence. We intended to count the baths—"They're bread and butter, you know," I solemnly informed the realtors. We had only a relatively small sum of money to apply as a down-payment. And we were going to ask one of the two Nantucket banks to underwrite the mortgage on whatever place we decided to buy.

If there is any species even more some sharp than a Nantucket realtor, not to mention infinitely more some cautious, it is a Nantucket banker. By "sharp," in both cases, I don't mean unethical. Quite the contrary. I mean a combination of alert, astute, and never asleep to the possibility of making an honest dollar—or preferably several thousand. It is an exaggeration to state—as some persons have done—that Nantucket bank tellers require the fingerprints of a depositor, for positive identification, before cashing a check. It is true, however, that even if you happen to be a teller's next-door neighbor, he will scrutinize you carefully—to make certain you are not an imposter—if the withdrawal is substantial.

One real-estate man, who had assured us that a certain little gold mine would be a steal for $40,000, didn't change his tune even when we told him we had only a few thousand dollars for a down-payment. He said that doubtless any mortgage company—or even better, some dear friend of ours—would be more than happy to lend us the difference, in view of the steal price. But the tune changed quickly when Bob pointed out we intended to give a local bank the opportunity of writing whatever mortgage we employed to effect the larceny.

Finally, we brought the realtor and a banker together for a conference.

"I know that house," nodded the banker—and of course the truth was that he knew *every* house. "We couldn't take anything but a small mortgage on it unless the foundation were completely rebuilt and the roof replaced."

"I mentioned the bad foundation and roof to them," said the realtor, not in the slightest abashed.

As a matter of fact, he *had* mentioned them, and in no uncertain terms. But somehow we had got the impression that the repairs would not be of a major nature. Well, after all, I suppose that if you are trying to sell a swaybacked horse, and at the same time to be honest, you point out that the horse is swaybacked. But you leave it up to the buyer to be alert enough to see whether the horse is so swaybacked that his stomach scrapes the ground.

At any rate, after that conference prices became more realistic, and the realtors didn't bother to show us places they knew we couldn't afford.

In being conducted through the few houses which were up for sale in the year-round part of town, Bob and I got a free sightseeing tour denied most off-islanders. And we *were* off-islanders, of course, in spite of Bob's accident of place of birth. By the law of averages, since there were a dozen in his family and since his mother had let nothing interfere with taking her growing family to Nantucket for the summers, at least one of the twelve would *have* to be born there.

In the year-round houses, we found some of the most beautiful antiques I had ever seen, as well as some of the most astounding bric-a-brac, china, and downright junk. Nantucketers seem to be even more reluctant than most New Englanders—and I come from a long line of string-savers—to throw away anything.

Occasionally they will give things away, though, for white elephant sales in the wintertime by churches. Our house-hunting tour convinced us there is ample stock on the island to supply a perpetual white elephant sale. There is little chance that the stock will be depleted, either, since what one islander gives away for the benefit of the church, some other islander buys for the benefit of the church—and husbands carefully, at least until the next white elephant sale.

Antiques, gimcracks, and scrimshaw—the spare-time carvings of sailing men—stood side by side in some of the houses which were for sale. Most islanders are well aware of the value of antiques, but occasionally a furnished house will turn out to be a real bargain because of one or two antique pieces.

I was tempted to buy one house simply because of an old and beautiful inlaid sideboard, probably brought originally from England, and a Colonial pine spice-cupboard, with eighteen tiny drawers arranged in tiers of three. But, fortunately, Bob remembered about bathrooms, and there were only two of them. To get from a front, second-story bedroom to a bath—without going through someone else's bedroom—entailed a trip down the front stairs and up the back stairs. Perhaps one reason I wanted the sideboard was so that I could smash some of the china it displayed, including one crockery vase, with cupids and the inscription "Souvenir of Mammoth Cave, Ky."

In another house, the front hall boasted a splendid antique grandfather's clock, a Colonial hooked rug, which should have been hanging in a museum, and a frightful Victorian what-is-it which served as a mirror, hatrack and bench.

As I have pointed out, Nantucket architecture escaped the Victorian invasion. The islanders, having lost their whaling industry, were lucky enough to be poor at the right time and didn't tear down their Colonial homes to make room for the expensive gingerbread monstrosities of the 'Nineties.

But a good deal of Victorian furniture found its way into Nantucket homes, just the same, and today's islanders are much too thrifty to throw it away or use it for kindling wood.

Bathrooms Are Bread and Butter

A super-salesman for the mirror-hatrack-bench combination must have passed through Nantucket sixty or seventy years ago, because we saw a number of the pieces in the homes and inns we inspected. The pieces are ornate and from a distance resemble a carved and armless throne with a huge backrest. The main part of the thing that looks like a backrest is a mirror. Curlicues, extending antler-fashion from the mirror frame, form hooks for hats and coats. A hole in the center of what looks like the throne's seat is for umbrellas and walking sticks. There is a brass can below to catch drippings from the umbrellas.

Bob said he'd like to own one just so that he could throw darts at it.

Obviously, it is a multi-purpose device. And we saw one which, judging by the fact that the umbrella hole had been enlarged considerably and made oval in shape, had at one time been pressed into service for still another use, perhaps not contemplated by its designer.

The scrimshaw, fashioned with infinite patience in forecastles and on pitch-smeared decks, was indescribably delicate and beautiful. There were walking sticks, windmills, bobbins, fans made from whalebone, figurines made from whales' teeth.

At the other extreme, and often in the same parlor, were some of the most hideous electric lamps ever to result from Mr. Edison's invention. Although certainly not antiques, they must be collectors' items—and Nantucket is full of them. They feature glass shades on which are painted waterfalls, lush pastoral scenes, and views of the Grand Canyon. A fringe in conservative scarlet or gold or both usually forms a skirt for the bottom of the shades, and the body of the lamp itself is apt to be a crockery parrot or kitten in improbable colors.

Many Nantucketers have impeccable taste about home furnish-

43

ings, and rely solely on beautiful antiques. But those homes weren't for sale, and perhaps never will be.

Bob, who took quite literally the "How To" books we had read about house-buying, always disappeared up into the attic or down into the foundations to poke into timbers with a jackknife and to scrape the surfaces of pipes to determine their condition. That left me with the "lady of the house" to hear rather thorough biographical sketches, of the former owners and original builders.

If there is a dwelling on Nantucket whose timbers weren't hewed from virgin New England forests, under the personal supervision of a whaling captain—usually named Coffin, Folger, Starbuck or Macy—and then brought to the island so that he could build a snug house for his bride—usually named Macy, Starbuck, Folger or Coffin—we didn't see it.

One woman, who had converted her house into an inn and who had a ten o'clock curfew after which she locked out her guests for the night, knew the history of her place down to the hand-wrought H hinges on the doors.

She said the hinges, which really were beautiful, came originally from the general store of a certain Mark Coffin, a school master turned prosperous merchant, who wanted to become an author.

"He moved from Nantucket town out to the moors," she related, "so that he wouldn't be interrupted in his writing. He liked it so well out there that he sold his store and gave his Nantucket home to the town to be used as a poorhouse. Well, it appears he couldn't sell anything that he wrote, and he finally ended up as a town charge in his own poorhouse."

She pointed out that her inn had four bathrooms, but when we went through the process of pacing from her nine bedrooms to the closest bath we discovered that three baths could be entered only through someone else's bedroom. That would mean three rooms with private baths and six rooms sharing the same bath. We knew that wouldn't do.

In the course of our tour, we also discovered that the old-fashioned kerosene stove—almost always in the living room and usually obstructing an old and beautiful fireplace—is a permanent Nantucket fixture.

I suppose it wasn't deliberate on the part of the realtors, but all of the homes and inns we were shown seemed part of a pattern to prepare us psychologically for the inn we were destined to buy.

Most of the homes could not possibly have been converted into inns. And most of the inns were far from ideal and were priced too high.

And then one realtor said he had just the place for us, Anchor Inn, on Centre Street. We didn't remember the inn itself, but we knew Centre Street and the location was ideal for our purpose.

He drove us there in his car, creeping the final block along a street which is so narrow that cars have to park with the right-hand wheels up on the sidewalk, and even then leave room enough for only one line of traffic.

"It's a lovely old Colonial house," the realtor said. "And it's a going business—it's been operating as an inn for over forty years."

He pulled up in front of a three-story, shingled house, painted the color of Guernsey cream and trimmed with bright-green shutters. Anchor Inn crowded the sidewalk, as do most old Nantucket homes, and was flanked by a white picket fence. English boxwood and lilac trees dotted the well-kept lawn. Bob and I knew it was what we had been looking for, and we nudged each other while attempting to keep our faces carefully non-committal.

We filed into the narrow front hall, and the place had a charm

45

all its own. Steep narrow steps led from the hall to the second floor. A little living room, with white panels covering a whole wall around a fireplace, opened off the hall. And the living room was furnished with wonderful antiques!

"Oh, Bob," I sighed, "it's just exactly . . ."

Bob elbowed me sharply, and glared.

"Yes, isn't it!" the realtor beamed.

". . . just exactly eleven minutes after one o'clock," I finished lamely.

"How many baths does it have?" Bob demanded.

"They're bread and butter, you know," I said brightly.

We walked all through Anchor Inn, and went through the formality of pacing from bedrooms to bathrooms. There were sixteen rooms and seven baths. We were gratified to note that it was possible to get from each bedroom to a bath without going through someone else's bedroom, descending a flight of stairs, climbing any trellises, or negotiating a widow's walk. Also, there were sinks in some of those bedrooms which didn't have their own private baths.

But I think we would have wanted to buy it if there were no baths at all, because both of us had been trapped and captured as soon as we saw it from the street.

Bob gave some of the beams and rafters the jackknife test, and—when we were out of earshot of the realtor—pronounced them to be every bit as sound as when they were cut from the heart of virgin New England forest.

The price was more than we had expected to pay for an inn, but Anchor Inn was more than we had hoped for. We told the realtor that there was just a slight possibility we might be interested, and that we'd think it over.

Bathrooms Are Bread and Butter

After Bob and I were back at The Shoe, we realized we had been so intent on remaining unenthusiastic that we didn't have the slightest idea of what Anchor Inn really looked like, inside or out. We drew separate floor plans, of how we remembered the interior, and they bore no resemblance to each other. We debated whether we should drive past the inn and have another look at the outside. But we were afraid the realtor might get wind of it and assume that we were eager to buy. So we decided to wait until dark. Then we figured and refigured the price, and all the time we were afraid that some other potential customer might be looking at Anchor Inn at that very moment, and beat us to the sale.

That night, we parked our car a block away from Centre Street, and nonchalantly strolled by the inn. The front door was only a couple of steps from the sidewalk, and we tiptoed up and had a close look at it.

A brass knocker, in the shape of an anchor, was fastened to the door.

"I don't care what the books say you should do before you buy a house," I whispered to Bob, "I want this one."

"Just like a woman!" Bob reproved me. "Ready to jump into the biggest financial transaction of your life without any sort of an investigation at all! We've got to go into this thing carefully." He lit his cigarette lighter to have a look at the door. "See what it says here on *our* knocker, honey?" he asked me excitedly. "Look, it's etched in the metal—'Anchor Inn.'"

Much as we wanted the inn and much as we feared that someone would buy it out from under us, we simply did not have the capital to make a large enough down-payment on the asking price.

Bob and I stayed up all that night trying to arrive at an offering

47

figure which would not insult the owner but would still leave us some margin for upward bargaining compromises.

When dawn came, I fixed breakfast and urged Bob to get Mr. Jordan, the realtor, on the telephone. But Bob insisted we should wait until the realtor called us. We sat there, waiting for the phone to ring and too nervous to read or listen to the radio, until almost noon. When the telephone finally jangled, Bob was careful to let it ring four times before he answered it.

"Hello," he said. "Yes, this is Robert Gilbreth." He nodded enthusiastically to me, and waved a crossed finger. "Who? I'm sorry, I'm afraid I still didn't get your name. Oh, yes, Mr. Jordan. It's good of you to call. We were just going out to see if we couldn't find some more inns for sale. What? Well, we really hadn't given it much more thought. I'll ask my wife."

Bob held the telephone where Mr. Jordan would be sure to hear the conversation, and shouted:

"It's Mr. Jordan, Barb. He's the real-estate man, remember? He wants to know whether we are still at all interested in that inn he showed us yesterday on Centre Street—what's its name? Mooring or Anchor or something like that."

Bob blocked off the mouthpiece so that whatever I said couldn't be heard. Actually, I didn't say anything, but Bob waited a few moments to give the impression he was listening to my words of wisdom. Then, taking his hand off the mouthpiece, he shouted again to me: "Well, that's about the way I feel, too. Luke warm. Of course, if they'd cut the price about in half, we might take it off their hands."

I don't think Mr. Jordan was fooled by Bob's deafening conversation with me. The realtor had probably been through countless similar situations, and besides, Bob has a tendency to over-act his thespian performances. Still, as I say, we had an argument that no amount of Yankee trading could budge—we simply didn't possess the money for a larger down-payment and we knew that Nantucket banks usually will write a mortgage for only sixty per-cent or less of the sale price.

We made an offer that was laughingly relayed to the owner and rejected. The owner made a new lower-priced offer that was relayed to us and laughingly rejected. Nantucket bankers were re-consulted about the mortgage. While there was no laughter from the bankers, and they agreed that Anchor Inn was a sound structure, they rejected any thought of departing from their mort-gage policies.

Mr. Jordan told us that other people were interested in buying Anchor Inn and we told him that we had heard of another inn which we believed we might like much better—over on Martha's Vineyard. Then he drove along Centre Street one day and caught us "strolling" by Anchor Inn. We made believe we were hurrying up town to do some marketing.

And, finally, we were only five hundred dollars apart on the price.

"The 'How To' books say," Bob told me, "that it is best to hold out for your own price, when your own price is all you can afford to pay. I say, let's split the difference."

That suited me and the owner. A meeting was arranged in the Town Building, attended by us, the owner, the realtor, three men from the bank, a lawyer, the register of deeds, and nine or ten town employees who had assembled to have a look at the young couple which "aimed to go into the 'roomah' business."

Bob had lectured me on the importance of our reading all the fine print, but it would have taken most of the morning to do so. Besides, we were much too jittery to concentrate in that room full of people. Finally we gave up all pretense of knowing what

49

was going on, and simply signed where we were told to. Checks were passed, papers shown, stamps affixed, and seals imprinted with such amazing skill and speed that Bob and I were bewildered when we emerged from the building a few minutes later.

"I wouldn't be surprised," Bob complained as we headed toward Anchor Inn with a pocketful of keys, "if we hadn't just finished selling Ann into indentured servitude to the owner, given Mr. Jordan the title to our car, and given the bank permanent possession of The Shoe and the two lighthouses."

Fortunately, we were dealing with people who, while thoroughly enjoying a horse-trading session, had complete integrity once the bargain had been concluded. So Ann didn't end up being an indentured servant.

We had an opportunity to make only a quick inspection of Anchor Inn, before we headed back to the mainland. Our vacations were over, and we intended to remain in Bloomfield and keep our jobs until the following summer.

The inn more than lived up to our expectations, as we hurried from room to room. But the speed of the transactions at the Town Building remained in Bob's mind.

"I never saw people so eager to get you to sign your life away," he kept repeating. "Everyplace I looked, someone had a blotter and was waiting on me to finish writing. I'll bet we could have got the inn for less money, if we had held out longer."

Actually, the price was fair. And if we had held out longer, someone else might have bought Anchor Inn. But on the steamer trip home, the question of whether we should have split that last five hundred dollars figured almost as prominently in our conversation as another even more important question: Whether

Ann would recognize her parents after their two-week absence.

I thought she might. Bob confidently expected his three-month-old daughter to greet him with open arms, hug him, and call him "Daddy."

4~ Screening Reservations

Almost as soon as we were settled down again in our Bloomfield apartment, we started receiving advance inquiries about reservations for the following summer. These letters, addressed to the inn, were forwarded to us by the Nantucket Post Office. Bob and I hung over our mailbox as eager as any budding author who has just sent his first epic to some fortunate publisher.

A typing course I had taken in high school stood me in good stead when it came to answering these inquiries. After we got home at night from our jobs, Bob and I collaborated in painstakingly drafting our glowing replies. We knew that, since we had somewhat over-extended ourselves financially, the mortgage payments would hinge on our keeping the inn full of guests. We intended to get as many firm reservations as possible from the tentative inquiries.

Some of the notes asked for information about Nantucket, and some for information about our accommodations. We studied the letters carefully, trying to size up the people who had written them. But we were generally unable to reach any conclusion except that nine out of ten persons don't put enough "m's" in accommodations.

I devised a standard reply to inquiries about vacationing at Nantucket. I worked on it for more than a week, and Bob said the Chamber of Commerce of the Garden of Eden would not have been ashamed of it. The inquiries about Anchor Inn sometimes could also be handled with a standard reply, covering our rates, distance from the bathing beaches, and accessibility to restaurants. Unlike many New England resort hotels and inns, we would use the European plan—on the grounds that it would be easier for us and that our guests would enjoy visiting various restaurants. We would serve breakfast "on request," but no other meals.

We also had a standard reply for people who wanted to know whether they could bring their household pets. The problem here was to tell them they couldn't, and still try to get across the impression that we sympathized with their request and had a warm spot in our hearts for animal lovers. Bob drafted an excellent letter which said, in part:

"We regret sincerely that, because some guests object to dogs, cats, parrots, canaries, rabbits, chinchillas (cross out all but one), we have been forced to adopt an inflexible rule against (insert species of pet), for business reasons. We ourselves are extremely fond of (insert species), especially (insert breed of species, if it has been mentioned in letter of inquiry). In fact, it was with a great deal of sorrow that we had to forego the pleasure and satisfaction of ever owning our own (insert species) when we became the proprietors of Anchor Inn. However, if you are still interested in making a reservation, we feel sure we could find boarding accommodations for your (insert species) within easy walking distance of our inn, so that you could visit together as often as you wished."

A number of other inquiries demanded special treatment, although I made carbons of each and found that I could sometimes use the same wording over again.

Yes, we have good mattresses and box springs . . . Yes, we have grass and flowers around the house, and both of us love grass and flowers . . . No, we don't have a curfew hour—we leave the front door unlocked and guests can come in as late as they please . . . Certainly, you can have the same room as last year, if you tell us which room you had and make your reservations far enough in advance . . . Yes, we allow children—in fact we have a lovely little girl of our own . . . Sorry to hear that your husband has not been feeling well. Certainly, we can let you have a room on the first floor . . . Yes, we have a few rooms with private baths . . . Yes, we can give you two bureaus . . . No, we don't have television . . . Yes, it will be all right to break your stay in the middle for two days while you fly home for Aunt Cora's Golden Wedding Anniversary. Isn't it splendid when two people stay happily married for so long . . . No, we don't have a bar, and perhaps you would feel more at home at one of the hotels . . . Yes, you can bring a portable radio . . . No, we are not surrounded by poison ivy and, having once been covered from head to foot with it myself, I certainly can sympathize with you . . . No, I don't know Nantucket's death rate, but if you will excuse an old joke I suspect that it is the same as any place else—one to a person. Seriously, it is an extremely healthy climate . . . No, we don't have organized games or floor shows . . . Yes, we have town drinking water and do not rely on our own well.

In each reply, we enclosed a printed picture of Anchor Inn.

For months, the letters of inquiry trickled in, without a single firm reservation, as Bob and I became increasingly apprehensive. But then we had a warm day in March, and two days later we received three reservations in the mail. Thereafter, following each warm spell, the reservation letters arrived. A good many of them came from persons who had first sent letters of inquiry, so we felt that the time devoted to drafting the replies had been well spent. It turned out that, from two hundred and fifty-four inquiries, we booked sixty-eight reservations—somewhat better than twenty-five per cent. We also received a number of other reservation requests from persons who didn't bother to write initial letters of inquiry.

But the reservation notes posed a new problem: Which to accept and which to reject.

There is no real formula for detecting—simply from a letter—a prudish old hen who is going to allege that her maidenly sensibilities are irretrievably compromised when she finds a pair of male pajama bottoms in a bathroom which she shares.

At the opposite side of the scale, there is no way of detecting—again simply from a letter—a gay old rooster whose "wife" will turn out to be a flashy hennaed job in yellow slacks, chest-happy sweater, and cow-belled ankle bracelets.

Both ends of the scale mean trouble. Put the old gal in a room separated from the suspected love nest by only a thin wall, and you are practically inviting the Decency League to swoop down on your establishment.

Persons who are experienced in running an inn develop a sixth sense in handling reservations. Also, they can hang out a figurative "No Vacancy" sign for those guests who had proved undesirable in the past.

But we had neither a sixth sense nor a knowledge of previous guests. Since we had no way of screening the reservations, and since we had to keep the inn as full as possible, we decided to accept all requests.

For the benefit of those who may some day contemplate operation of a summer inn, I will say that our experience has proved the best bet is the reservation which arrives on office stationery, dictated by a businessman who wants accommodations for himself and his wife. When a man writes on his firm's letterhead, and additionally confides his plans to his secretary, it is almost certain that he is neither seeking a love nest nor planning to defray his holiday expenses by subsequently auctioning off the sheets and towels that he has stolen from you. Another good bet is a reservation on printed stationery, with a home address, signed by the lady of the house.

The worst bet—although I can't imagine why—is precise, small handwriting on expensive but unengraved and unprinted writing paper. If the return address on such writing paper happens to be general delivery, the best policy is to drop the letter in a wastebasket and pretend you never received it.

On the other hand, some of our most pleasant guests have been persons whose reservation requests were all but illegible scribbles on postal cards.

In no case, though, sixth sense or not, can any *positive* conclusion be drawn from a reservation request by a stranger. The businessman who confides his plans to his secretary, for instance, conceivably can be planning a little commandment-breaking with the secretary herself.

Bob and I were determined to do our best to have no commandment-breaking. We didn't subscribe to it, and addition-

57

ally thought it would be bad for business. Since Anchor Inn's biggest asset is its quiet atmosphere, we knew it would be wise to cater only to conservative people.

But you can't very well write a letter telling a prospective guest not to come if he isn't conservative.

Once we had confirmed all the reservations, there wasn't anything we could do about the situation except to worry. And Bob said he would leave that chore to me, since I was so good at it.

Meanwhile, ending a secret shared only with our families, we gave notice to our landlord that we would soon be moving out of the apartment, and to our bosses that we would soon be quitting our jobs. In order to cut down the interval of our "unemployment," we planned to keep our jobs until the end of May, and then move immediately to Nantucket and get the inn ready to open within a few days.

My friends were unanimously envious, when they heard the news. They seemed to picture me as the mistress of a large corps of servants, who would do all the work around the inn, bring me my morning coffee in bed, and double as baby sitters for Ann while I relaxed on the beach.

"What fun you're going to have picking out new curtains for all those bedrooms!" a girl who lived in an apartment near ours kept reminding me. "And when you feel like a snack or anything like that, all you'll have to do is clap your hands and get room service."

Bob's friends, on the other hand, thought he should have his head examined. Some of them were of the opinion that running a quaint establishment for tourists was intimately associated with certain types of handle-bearing, old-fashioned crockery, formerly found under beds. A few of the comics in Bob's office amused themselves by filing past his desk while carrying wastebaskets at arm's length as if they were performing a disagreeable chore. Their ideas of summer inns might have been accurate forty years ago. Today it is not the crockery object but a pipe-unstopping implement, known as the plumber's friend, with which the inn proprietor is on familiar terms.

Some of Bob's friends also implied that running an inn—while not quite the same as operating a lavender-and-old-lace tea room, an interior-decorating salon, or a dress-designing business—was a less manly occupation than commuting to and from New York with the virile suburban crowd.

There also were some forecasts that we'd starve to death, and that Bob would probably be coming back to New York, hat-in-hand, after the current season.

"That shows how much they know," Bob grumbled as he relayed these predictions to me. "If they had any power of observation, they'd know very well that I never wear a hat."

On the day Bob finally left his job, he drove up to my family's place in Somers, Connecticut, and borrowed a farm truck from my father. Leaving our car in Somers, Bob returned with the truck to Bloomfield and prepared to load it with our clothes and furniture.

I had endorsed this plan for minimizing freight expenses. Even though I knew Bob had never driven a truck before, I also had agreed that Ann and I would ride in the truck with him from Bloomfield to Woods Hole.

However, when I saw the truck and the way Bob was loading it, I privately made up my mind that Ann and I would never set foot in it. Although entirely serviceable, the borrowed vehicle was far from new. Even a hasty glance revealed that it had been used for various agrarian activities, including the recent hauling of livestock. While it undoubtedly was a big asset on my father's farm, it did nothing to decorate our residential street in Bloomfield.

When Bob finished loading all of our furniture that would fit in, the truck resembled to the last bucket and mattress a stage prop for Mr. Steinbeck's *Grapes of Wrath*. All it needed, up there in the cab, were the driver's dusty wife and a crying year-old child.

"I don't dare pile the stuff any higher," said Bob, looking ruefully at a small stack of our furniture still standing at the curb. "I may have to let a little air out of the tires to get the truck on the steamer, as it is."

It goes without saying that Bob knew, to the inch, the dimensions of steamer's opening, through which he was going to have to drive.

"That'll be quite a job—to maneuver this thing onto the steamer," he continued. "Also, I'm not looking forward to driving through New York traffic."

"You mean," I gulped, "you're going to try to drive it through New York *City?*"

"That's the shortest way. Then I'll have to fight out the Boston Post Road traffic, since trucks aren't allowed on the parkways. And then, as I say, will come the real fun—running it up the gangplank. I suppose they'll make me back it on, so that I can get it off easier."

I was trying to think up a good, logical excuse why Ann and I would find it impossible to accompany him. But then Bob himself saved me the trouble.

"Look, honey," he asked, "would it disappoint you a whole lot if I drove the truck to Nantucket without you? I could get the rest of the furniture in the cab, if I drove it up by myself."

"So that's why I'm getting all the build-up about heavy traffic

and driving onto the boat," I replied, having found out that it
was wise always to win a point reluctantly from Bob. "Do you
mean to tell me you want to leave Ann and me here without any
furniture?"

"Oh, no, not that," he reassured me. "You and Ann take a bus
up to Somers, and wait for me there. I'll return the truck to your
father the day after tomorrow, and pick up you and Ann and the
car."

"I don't know," I stalled. "A bus trip with a baby isn't much
fun and . . ."

"You could take a plane," Bob suggested. "Or, if you're dead
set on going with me, I guess we could send the rest of the furniture by express."

"I'll gladly help you load it into the cab," I agreed hastily.

Aside from losing three bureau drawers on the George Washington Bridge, and the bureau someplace between Bridgeport and
New Haven, Bob's trip to and from Nantucket was practically
uneventful. So was Ann's and mine to Somers, and our subsequent trip to Nantucket with Bob.

It was wonderful to realize, when we moved into Anchor Inn,
that we were in business together, that we were working for
ourselves, that there wouldn't be any more commuting, and above
all that we were on Nantucket.

5 ~ Laundryman

Nantucket in early June was crisply cool, dew drenched, lettuce green, and beautiful. Only a handful of summer people had arrived, and we ourselves had no reservations booked for a week. However, we thought there was a chance we might pick up a guest or two—off the street, so to speak—in the intervening period.

We had come in on the afternoon steamer, and immediately tackled two of the front guest rooms. We gave them a hasty sweepdown, dusting, and airing, and then Bob ran the vacuum while I made the beds. I had read in a magazine about an efficient method of bed-making, wherein you start at the bottom tucking in all your sheets and blankets, and even the bedspread, and then work up the sides. I had practiced this on our own bed in Bloomfield during the winter, and had become fairly skilled at it. I had the beds in the two rooms made up long before Bob finished with the vacuum.

63

Just before dark, Bob put up the Anchor Inn sign in front of our house, indicating that we were open for business. We turned on the front light, and as an afterthought turned on lights in a number of the bedrooms, to give the impression that guests already had sought us out. This wasn't designed to impress the neighbors, but to make room-seeking tourists think they had stumbled on a popular and desirable haven.

Then, while hoping for the best, we finally got around to getting our own bedroom for occupancy.

Our light-burning strategy didn't land us any guests, and it was perhaps just as well. We had a tremendous amount of work to do, and the guests would have been underfoot and perhaps uncomfortable.

The whole island of Nantucket, meanwhile, was a scene of frantic activity which reminded me of our Four-Town Fair in Connecticut, the day before the gates are opened to the public.

Jobs that should have been done months before—but that no one had got around to—were being rushed to slap-dash completion. Painters, plumbers, roofers, and carpenters, as well as people who *said* they were painters, plumbers, roofers, and carpenters, were getting the summer cottages ready for occupancy. Tiny sailboats and small yachts were being calked, painted, and rolled into the water. Wooden planks and faded newspapers were being torn down from the display windows in many of the stores. Shutters were being opened and storm doors removed from restaurants and tourist homes. Everybody was in a hurry—a condition which, as we found out later, occurs on the island only once a year, and lasts for a period of not more than a couple of weeks.

In spite of the hectic bustle, our arrival was not overlooked. The fact that the new owners had arrived at Anchor Inn was duly recorded, with satisfying detail, by *The Nantucket Town Crier*

and the blanket-sized *Inquirer and Mirror,* both of which splendid
publications are read from masthead to want ads by every literate
Nantucketer.

The result was that our house-opening activities for the next
week were often interrupted by Nantucket callers, who usually
found me in a dirty house dress, sneakers, and towel fashioned
into a dust cap.

All of these callers seemed to be well-meaning, intensely ob-
servant, and outstanding authorities on how to operate an inn.
Many of them had some sort of summer business, and hoped
we would steer our guests to their taxicabs, sightseeing buses,
sailboats, restaurants, and bicycles-for-hire shops. They left us
enough advertising material to stock the Waldorf-Astoria in New
York.

One lady endeared herself to me by saying that she'd come to
call on my mother. When I explained that my mother was in
Somers, she added that, at any rate, she'd like to see the "lady
of the house."

"I'm the lady of the house," I declared, removing my dust cap
and inviting her in.

"Do you mean a girl your age is going to try to run this inn?"
she asked. "I hope you know what you're doing."

I hoped so, too.

A good portion of our callers rented rooms to summer people.
Although they must have been as busy getting ready for the season as we were, they managed to find time to come over and size
up their competition, while additionally giving the once-over to
possible new members of the year-round community.

The attitude of at least one room-renter, a friendly middle-aged
woman named Mrs. Williams, seemed to be that paying guests
were a necessary evil which, while tolerated, should not be in-

dulged. She advised me not to knock myself out with house-cleaning.

"You'll find," she asserted, "that no matter how hard you work you won't get many guests until the peak of the season, from the middle of July to the end of August. And at the peak of the season, you'll get more guests than you can handle. So, I say, let them shift for themselves."

"Do you tell them to make their own beds and all?" I asked.

"Not exactly," she grinned. "I have a sign in my parlor saying that because of the pressure of other duties, the management doesn't aim to make any beds or clean any rooms after eight o'clock in the morning."

"But people surely don't get out of their rooms by eight o'clock!"

"I'll own up to that," she said. "And when they finally do get out of their rooms *after* eight, I let them make their own beds and I leave a dust mop propped up against their door. Sort of a gentle hint."

"And you still get guests?"

"During the rush season, *everybody* gets guests. I've heard tell," she chuckled, "that some mainlanders are so hard up for places to go they even visit Martha's Vineyard during the rush season, although it beats me why."

But our most impressive visitor was a Mrs. Macy, sometimes referred to as Widow Macy, to distinguish her from a daughter-in-law who was Mrs. Doctor Macy. Mrs. Macy, the widow, was in her seventies, corpulent, and uncompromisingly corseted. She arrived wearing a black, ankle-length dress; starched bodice; high, black, Ground-Gripper shoes, with medium-height heels; and an old-rose, crocheted, handsome, something-or-other which resembled both a hug-me-tight and a sleeveless Eisenhower jacket, and which actually is known on Nantucket as a waumus.

Mrs. Macy bore a platter of cookies, most of which she proceeded to devour herself. Despite her excess weight and fondness for her own cooking, she was a woman of great dignity, with intelligent eyes and a cultured voice which she never raised above a half-whisper.

She examined us carefully, and apparently found us wanting. She was far too much of a lady not to observe the social amenities, but even while doing so her lips were pressed together in close, if flabby, disapproval. After the amenities, she delivered her opening gambit from the delicate and dangerously sagging amidships of the beautiful Victorian sofa in our living room-lobby. The gambit did little to set our minds at rest about our reservation list.

"I hope," she said skeptically in her cultured half-whisper, "that you children plan to run a *respectable* place."

I assured her at some length that we did. She nodded, as if that was exactly what she expected me to say—and as if, of course, she knew better than to believe a word of it.

It developed that Mrs. Macy ran an inn within a few doors of ours, and that she did not propose to see the neighborhood go to pot.

"I assume that *all* of your guests won't arrive from the mainland in trucks from Oklahoma," she declared.

"From Oklahoma?" I inquired. "Oh, I guess you mean the truck we borrowed to bring down some of our furniture. It came from Connecticut, as a matter of fact, not Oklahoma."

Mrs. Macy dismissed that detail of geography with a wave of her hand. "I am *sure,*" she said, and again the implication was that she was sure of something just the opposite, "that you have gone through your reservations carefully, so as to discourage the wrong sort of people from coming to Nantucket."

"Just as carefully as we knew how," I replied quite truthfully, squirming under her sharp scrutiny. I wished she'd look at Bob a while, instead of me. But I seemed to be the specimen in which she was principally interested. To change the subject, I asked hopefully: "Wouldn't you like us to show you around the inn? We're getting it just as neat as a pin."

"I know every inch of it," said Mrs. Macy. "Under the former owner, it *always* was a respectable place."

"And it still is. And it still will be," I stammered, favoring her with what I hoped was a sincere smile. "Won't it, Bob?" I asked desperately.

Bob had the bad taste to snigger at my discomfort. "Good cookies," he affirmed.

"It will be *some* respectable," I added, deciding to fall back on the Nantucket superlative. Mrs. Macy was smart enough to know that I was imitating her fellow townsmen, and apparently she considered that a license to which I was not entitled. She frowned her disapproval. "Won't it be respectable, Bob?" I begged.

"If you say so, dear," said Bob, electing to torture me by playing the role of the henpecked husband who had fallen in with his wife's nefarious schemes. "Yes, indeedy."

"You'll find I'm a direct person," Mrs. Macy told me. "We may as well get matters shipshape from the start. I won't put up with neighbors who are not respectable."

"I certainly don't blame you," I said. "No, sir. Not at all. You don't blame her either, do you Bob?"

"I'm afraid I wasn't paying any attention, my love," said Bob in feigned apology. "Would you repeat that question, please?"

It wouldn't have taken much for me to crown him over the head with the cookie platter.

"My inn is my living," Mrs. Macy continued. "I don't hold with

68

noisy and disreputable people and I don't aim to have them on this block. If you people don't run a taut inn, I'll go to the police. I've done it before."

I said I was sure she had. Frankly, I was scared to death of her, and I didn't want her to get back on the subject of whether we had screened our reservations.

Bob adores most characters, especially elderly female ones who don't happen to be staying at our inn. For some reason which is hard to fathom, since he doesn't go out of his way to be particularly agreeable to them, they seem to like him, too. Maybe his secret of success with the old girls is that, instead of treating them as inhibited museum pieces, he likes to needle them and even shock them a little. At any rate, Bob now decided it was time to deal himself into the conversation.

"I don't doubt that you know every inch of the place," he told Mrs. Macy, "but you haven't seen what my wife has done to the attic. That's where we're going to put the bar and roulette wheels."

"The *what?*" gasped Mrs. Macy.

"And the girls," Bob leered, "will be on the second floor. I'm not exaggerating, Mrs. Macy, when I tell you we've managed to get some real pips. My wife thought . . ."

"Whatever she thought," Mrs. Macy quivered indignantly, but still in her half-whisper, "she calculated wrong, mister. Nantucket doesn't hold with those sort of doings."

"Now don't go judging our girls until you see them," Bob advised her patiently. "These girls have real class. Now the crap tables . . ."

"I don't want to hear another word," Mrs. Macy declared, "especially about tables of that kind. And if you . . ."

While I was contemplating the wisdom of hiding under the sofa, and immediately rejecting the idea because there wasn't adequate space beneath the sag she was creating, Mrs. Macy broke off in mid-sentence and suddenly beamed at Bob.

"You young rascal," she said, obviously delighted, "I ought to box your ears. You *are* twitting me, aren't you?"

"I'm twitting you," Bob conceded, "because that's the kind of a place you implied we were going to run."

"Have another cookie, boy," she urged him. "I said to myself when I first saw you that *she* probably doesn't feed you enough."

"I don't like to be the old maid," said Bob, in what I thought was a rather tactless reference to her appetite. "But I can't turn down a peace offering, even if it empties the plate."

"It's a peace offering," Mrs. Macy nodded.

"We may as well come clean, then," said Bob. "We're new at this business. We didn't know any way to screen our reservation requests, so we accepted them all."

"There wasn't much else you could do," she admitted.

"Well, frankly, we *are* a little concerned about keeping order," Bob confessed. "What do you suggest? What do you do yourself?"

Mrs. Macy's suggestions made sense. She said that if we remembered always to be extremely quiet and dignified, most of our guests would automatically follow suit. This would create an atmosphere which would be oppressive to the loud-talking, party-throwing type of individual, and he would move out of his own accord. If he failed to do so, he should be invited to leave. As for commandment-breakers:

"I send for the police," said Mrs. Macy.

"But suppose you only suspect, and aren't even sure?" I asked.

"In this business," said Mrs. Macy positively, and pressing her lips together again, "if you suspect you can be sure."

After she had gone, Bob and I talked over the matter of our own dignity. We both promised that we would try to be especially well behaved once the guests started to arrive.

"And no more twitting, you scamp, you," I warned him.

In the days that followed, while we worked to finish removing the accumulation of winter dust, we practiced on each other how we would greet our first guests. We soon mastered Mrs. Macy's half-whisper and well-modulated tones.

Bob and I scrubbed and waxed every inch of the floors and furniture, washed every window, and dusted all the walls, ceilings, and woodwork. We repainted the kitchen and cleaned the screens. We were also introduced to a phenomenon peculiar to seaside inns, which is that the wood in bureau drawers continues to grow each year, just as surely as if it were still rooted in its native habitat.

Almost every drawer in the place was stuck solidly to its bureau. Bob managed to extract some of the drawers by sitting on the floor, bracing his feet against the edges of the bureau, and tugging on the drawer-pulls. In general, though, this method extracted more drawer-pulls than it did drawers. A mallet and screwdriver were somewhat more effective, but a few drawers were stuck so solidly that it was necessary to dismantle entire bureaus.

Once the drawers were removed, Bob planed them down and rubbed the edges with soap, so that they'd slide easily. But by the middle of the season, many of them were stuck again, and by the following year they had grown solidly back into the framework.

The job of getting the inn ready was the first big project we had ever tackled together, and although the work was sometimes back-breaking we enjoyed it. There was an immense satisfaction in realizing that the inn and every stick of furniture was ours, or would be some day if we could pay our debts.

71

We hadn't examined the premises as closely as we should have when we decided to buy. But our inch-by-inch examination now more than pleased us. As the dust sheets came off the downstairs furniture, we discovered we were the owners of a beautiful, antique, apple-wood desk, brass candle sconces, a number of handsome hooked rugs, and two Colonial rockers. In the guests rooms were empire bureaus (with growing drawers), pine chests, spool beds and Chippendale mirrors with eagles resplendent in gilt. For the first few days, we spent almost as much time summoning each other to look at discoveries, as we did in working. I'd open up a cabinet and find some old pewter cups, and Bob would come racing down from the attic to view and appraise them.

Or he'd discover, as he scrubbed the painted floors on hands and knees, a particular plank which was almost two feet wide, and I'd come dashing to the scene with a ruler to see if that plank set a record for width in Anchor Inn. Where layers of paint on the floors were chipped, the wood showed through, mellow and old. Sanded down, the floors would be handsome, but that would have to wait until next year. I don't believe any inn was ever cleaner than ours, when the day finally came on which the first guests with reservations were scheduled to arrive. Having waited in vain for customers "off the street," Bob and I had started to wonder whether perhaps there wasn't something basically wrong with our inn. Since we hadn't required deposits with reservations, we weren't at all sure that our scheduled guests would show up.

We had reservations for nine people: Three married couples; one man, whether single or married we didn't know, but in any event he was coming by himself; and two women whose signatures had been preceded by a "(Miss)."

"Suppose," I asked Bob for the twentieth time, "that they've changed their plans and didn't bother to let us know. Suppose

one of those Misses in parentheses turns out to be—well, you know
—the sort of girl you were kidding Mrs. Macy about."

"Don't worry about it," said Bob, nervously pacing the floor.

"If they come at all, they'll probably all come on the afternoon
steamer," I told him. "Maybe we ought to ask Mrs. Macy to drop
over and size them up when they arrive."

"We're going to run this business ourselves, and we've got to
start sometime," Bob shook his head.

"Suppose," I said, "they come in, look around, and don't like the
place."

"I don't know," Bob groaned. "Let's dust the rooms again and
make sure everything is set. Then maybe they'll like it."

We dusted, although there was no dust. I put flowers in all the
vases. I hoped that Ann, who was ordinarily well behaved,
wouldn't pick that particular afternoon to raise the roof. We intended to keep her hidden for the next few days, because we were
afraid some of our guests might think she'd keep them awake,
and would decide not to stay. The afternoon boat got in at two-
thirty. Bob and I, waiting in the living room-lobby, were immacu-
late after what would be our final real baths for some time. "Is
the guest registration book ready?" Bob asked me in Mrs. Macy's
funereal whisper. "Is there ink in the fountain pen?"

"Everything has been laid out," I replied, and then tittered nervously as I realized I had fallen unconsciously into a funereal expression.

Bob scowled at this unseemly display of levity, and went over
to examine again the registration book.

"Do you think," he asked, "that if someone saw he was the
very first guest he might decide there was something the matter
with this place, and change his mind about staying?"

It took me two bounds to get to the desk and grab the pen.

"Give me some names," I urged Bob. "Any names at all. I'll write some of them backhand and some of them forehand and you can write some of them . . ."

Our doorbell interrupted me.

"Too late," Bob jittered. "We'll have to take a chance."

I put down the pen, having been saved by the bell from forgery, and we both went to the door. Bob opened it and bowed, and I stood one pace behind him with my right hand on my stomach and my left arm extended toward the living room, in a gracious gesture of hospitality.

"Welcome to Anchor Inn," Bob whispered formally. "We *hope* your stay will prove most enjoyable. I am Robert Gilbreth, and I would like to present my wife, Mrs. Gilbreth."

Our callers were an elderly couple, and I guess it would have been the last straw if they had rung the bell merely to seek directions to the bathing beach. When they introduced themselves, we recognized their names as one of the three couples which had made reservations.

They came into the front hall and Bob motioned them into the lobby.

"If you will be good enough to sign the registration book," he whispered, "it will be a pleasure to show you to your room."

"Is somebody sick?" the elderly gentleman asked.

"No, indeed," Bob assured him. "However, we try to maintain a quiet atmosphere."

"Good idea," the gentleman replied.

"If you'll just sign the registry," Bob urged.

"Let them start a new page," I suggested.

"Certainly," said Bob.

The gentleman signed, and we had our first two guests. Since it turned out that they weren't speaking to each other, we couldn't have asked for two quieter people. The elderly lady said she had a bad back, and would like a bedboard under her mattress if possible. There was one around someplace, and Bob went to fetch it. I showed them up to their room, helping with some of the light luggage. And all the time I was dreading that they'd say they didn't like the inn, and decide to go somewhere else.

They examined their room critically. Then the man glared at his wife, cleared his throat, and smiled pleasantly at me.

"It's a real pleasure after all these years," he said, "to be in a bedroom that is actually spotless."

"Indeed it is spotless, my dear," his wife assured me. "I'm sorry to say, though, that you may have a full-time job trying to *keep* it that way."

I knew I was meant to gather from him that his bedroom at home was a pigpen, and from her that he was the pig who kept it that way. Actually they were both meticulously neat, and cleaning their room at Anchor Inn was always a breeze.

After Bob arrived with the bedboard and installed it, he and I went back downstairs to wait for our next guests. Incidentally, we both forgot about the bedboard after the elderly couple checked out three weeks later, and it remained under the mattress for the rest of the season. Since the room was almost constantly occupied, I suppose some twenty guests ultimately departed firm in the belief that sleeping on a bed at Anchor Inn was like sleeping on the floor.

The other two couples we were expecting arrived almost simultaneously, a few minutes later. They were so obviously newlyweds that, even though we were green to the business, there was no mistaking them.

Bob's greeting began to sound like a whispered phonograph record:

"Welcome to Anchor Inn. (Pause) We *hope* your stay will prove *most* enjoyable. I am Robert Gilbreth . . ." And so forth.

The two honeymooning couples were so far in the clouds that they scarcely noticed us and didn't notice the inn at all.

The man who had asked for a single reservation turned out to be a Mr. Joseph Brownley, a middle-aged bachelor and department-store executive. We decided immediately that he was much too occupied with his own importance to have time for even the mildest of vices. Like the newlyweds, he didn't bother to pay any attention to us or the inn. He was primarily interested in our only telephone, situated in a hall next to the kitchen, and had to make three long-distance calls on business matters before he went up to his room. Despite the sign on the kitchen door, which at that time said "Private," Mr. Brownley kept the door propped open with his foot during all three calls. I can't guess why, unless he considered himself such a big wheel that private entrances constituted a sub-conscious challenge to his importance.

Bob finally showed him upstairs, and I answered the next ring of the doorbell. It was a jolly, heavy-set young woman—one of the two Misses in parentheses we were expecting. Since I couldn't improve on Bob's little speech, I copied it. Bob came downstairs and into the front hall just in time for me to announce that I was Barbara Gilbreth, and that I would like to present my husband, Mr. Gilbreth. This guest, a school teacher, was kind enough to exclaim that the inn was lovely. She stayed with us for two weeks, always made her own bed, liked to take Ann with her to the beach, and thought that a gay evening on the town consisted of a movie all by herself, followed by a banana split.

The last to arrive was the prim old spinster, Miss Thomas, whose morning egg had to be removed from the ice box the night before. Both Bob and I were on hand to greet her. Having gained confidence and having profited by practice, Bob now exuded poised dignity. He had dropped his voice half an octave, from baritone to bass, and was all but plagiarizing Mrs. Macy's modulations.

After listening to Bob's speech of welcome, Miss Thomas thoroughly supervised her cab driver, as he brought into our hall enough luggage for a triumphant tour of Europe. When the task was completed to her satisfaction, she tipped him a dime.

"You've *earned* it," she assured him.

Bob and I wrestled her luggage upstairs, with Bob making three trips. We had already decided that, being the owners, we wouldn't accept tips, and she seemed to approve when Bob rejected his dime.

Miss Thomas had to have the flowers, wool blanket, and rug whisked immediately out of her room, because they allegedly gave her hay fever. It is my personal opinion, though, that if we had originally shown her into a room without those articles, she would have said that it lacked color, looked bare, and that she resented our ill-concealed plot to freeze her to death.

All in all, though, Bob and I had reason to congratulate ourselves on our first batch of guests. There was not the slightest doubt that all of them were respectable. Even Mrs. Macy, who dropped over later that afternoon to see how we were doing, had to admit that from what she had observed from her front window, there seemed no immediate reason to summon the gendarmerie.

Besides being respectable, they were quiet. We heard scarcely a sound from them all that first afternoon. When they trickled out for supper, we noticed there was no clatter in the halls and no one allowed the front screen door to slam.

Bob attributed their quietness almost altogether to our own demeanor. We had been moving around practically on tiptoe, and hadn't yet abandoned Mrs. Macy's half-whisper. It was beginning to get on my nerves a little, but I couldn't argue with the successful results.

Ann cooperated by falling asleep right after supper. The guests started returning after eating in nearby restaurants, and went quietly to their rooms. The front doorbell, under which Bob had affixed a sign saying "Ring Bell for Manager," sounded once, but it didn't wake Ann and by the time Bob answered it, no one was there. I began setting the tables for breakfast, and Bob announced that he thought he'd go out to the laundry shed and iron for about half an hour.

Although more than pleased with the inn itself, I was not in the least pleased with the contents of the rustic-looking laundry shed, located in the back yard behind our tulip bed. The shed contained an apparently home-made gas water heater, a couple of sinks, a small washing machine that had to be kept operating on an eight-hour basis every day to keep up with the dirty sheets, and a huge, old, and tremendously complicated automatic ironer.

I am no expert in such matters, but I could tell that the ironer had been manufactured long before my time and was in a dangerous state of disrepair. The metal, rounded shoe of the device was heated with gas and the cloth-covered roller driven by electricity. Some of the gas jets were so hopelessly rusted that they wouldn't light at all. The remaining jets got so much gas they shot hissing flames eight inches long. When you tried to light the thing, the gas sometimes would blow out the match and sometimes explode in your face.

The electric motor, a sizeable and interesting antique, was connected to the ironer by a wide leather belt. To start the motor required both nerve and agility.

The first step was to throw an electric switch on the wall, and

Laundryman

it was the sort of switch in which I have no confidence. A hard-rubber handle was attached to two hinged copper prongs. The prongs had to be disengaged from one set of contacts and swung in a one-hundred-and-eighty-degree arc to engage another set of contacts.

Throwing the switch caused all of the lights in Anchor Inn to grow dim, while the motor hummed ominously and emitted smoky fumes, and the leather belt twitched like something alive. Maybe I've seen too many movies, but the whole thing always reminded me of an electrocution. As soon as the switch was thrown, it was necessary to leap across the room to the ironer and start spinning the cloth-covered roller by hand. This resulted in changing the motor's hum to a series of groans, delivered with the cadence of labor pains.

After vomiting violet sparks that made you wish for welder's goggles, the motor would slowly begin to revolve, pick up speed, stop smoking, stop vomiting, and allow the lights to come back bright again. Then it would settle down to a clacketty roar, while the belt popped viciously and the roller turned with a persistence so inexorable that if it had caught your hand I don't believe it would have let you go until your body was rolled flat.

After watching Bob's first encounter with the equipment, I had vowed that neither of us would ever go near it again. But Bob had ignored my warnings and my pleas, and seemed to have mastered the machinery of the ironer, if not the technique of ironing. On the trial runs that he made before our guests arrived, his sheets were usually wrinkled and sometimes scorched. Also, he possessed an uncanny ability for trapping moths, butterflies, june bugs and (once) a mouse within the pillow cases, immediately before running them through the ironer.

I am afraid that Bob had little or no natural talent for doing

79

laundry, despite his frequent claims that his sheets were shades whiter than those of anyone else on the block. If you could believe Bob, the whiteness of his laundry, when displayed on our clothes lines, was the envy of housewives up and down the island.

Even in subsequent years, when we managed to get new equipment, Bob's pillowcases sometimes contained insect corpses and his sheets sometimes were scorched and ripped. The corpses he dismissed fatalistically as the will of God. The scorches and rips he attributed to those thoughtless guests who presumably wore spurs while smoking in bed.

If I had had my way, Bob certainly would have stayed out of the laundry shed that particular night. Our luck had been so good, with all nine of our guests showing up on schedule, that I thought doing the ironing would be tempting fate.

"As a personal favor to me," I urged him, "don't do any laundry tonight."

"I'll just iron a dozen sheets or so," Bob whispered, "while you're setting the tables."

"Well, will you promise to be careful?"

"I won't make a sound," said Bob.

"I'm not thinking about the noise," I said, forgetting Mrs. Macy's restrained delivery. "I'm thinking about being a widow."

"Hush," Bob warned. "It's perfectly safe if a person knows what he's doing. Can I trust you not to clatter the dishes while you're setting the tables?"

I said I'd be quiet. Bob got a flashlight and departed for the shed. In the beam of the flashlight, I could see him—and this is the simple truth—tiptoe through the tulips.

I went back to setting the tables, but my mind was on Bob. I knew that, customarily, he started the electric motor before he lit the gas, so that the cloth-covered roller wouldn't be hot when he had to spin it by hand.

I could picture him standing by the switch and screwing up his nerve, while measuring carefully the distance he would have to leap between the switch and the roller. I waited tensely for the lights to grow dim. Instead they flickered twice, to the accompaniment of a hissing sound. Then, as a blue arc briefly lit up the back yard, the lights went out altogether.

I heard a couple of cries of dismay from upstairs, but my immediate concern was for Bob. I fumbled my way to the back door, and was gratified to see Bob and the flashlight coming through the tulip bed again.

Bob was furious, but he still remembered not to raise his voice.

"That motor's not going to make me lose *my* temper," he grated, "even if it did short out and knock me all the way across the blasted shed. No, sir. No motor's going to get *me* down."

"I forbid you to go back out there again," I whispered. "You stay away from that motor."

Bob pointed the flashlight beam at my face, so that he could observe the full effect of his next remark.

"One more peep out of you," he whispered, "and I'll iron you. Where's the fuse box?"

"How can I tell you if I'm not allowed to peep?" I asked, now as furious as he.

"Just tell me, and then stop peeping," he demanded.

The fuse box was up on the second floor, in a guest room. Luckily for Bob, the guest room was still vacant. It would have served him right if it had been the room we had given to Miss Thomas, the crabby spinster.

I explained where the box was located, and then stood there in the dark while he went upstairs with the flashlight. He soon had the lights going again. When he came downstairs, I noticed that aside from a burn on his left forearm, he was practically unmarked.

He started for the laundry shed, mumbling that no unmentionable ironer and no unmentionable, nagging wife were going to make him lose *his* temper or make him raise *his* voice. No sirree, he let it be known, the ironer and I had another think coming if we thought we were going to get *his* goat.

The truth was that, like an airplane pilot who insists on taking up another plane immediately after a crash, he knew that if he was ever going to tackle the ironer again he had to tackle it immediately, before he lost his courage.

I suppose I should have gone with him, to be ready to administer artificial respiration or something, in the event of further trouble. But I simply couldn't bring myself to watch him tinkering with the dangerous equipment. Besides, in his present mood, I wasn't absolutely sure he *wouldn't* try to iron me.

I paced the kitchen, waiting again for the lights to dim. The Big House illusion was strong now. I was on Death Row. At any moment the switch would be thrown and another dear colleague would have walked the Last Mile.

The lights went dim. I heard the hum of the motor and its labor pains as Bob spun the roller. Then the lights came back bright and the motor settled down to its roar. I breathed a sigh of relief, but I knew there was still one more hurdle: Lighting the gas which heated the ironer's shoe.

I remember exactly how Bob did it. He set fire to a long taper of newspaper, gingerly turned on the gas, got as far away from the ironer as possible, and then dropped the newspaper on the shoe while leaping for safety. This was usually accompanied by a fairly loud pop. I strained my ears for it.

And then the noise came, with a sheet of flame. And instead of being a mere pop, it was a window-rattling explosion.

I was about to rush to the rescue, when from the interior of the laundry shed came Bob's voice—no longer muted in Mrs. Macy's refined whisper. His voice, bellowing at foghorn intensity, was making the improbable assertion that the ironer had sprung, already revolving, from the vitals of a female dog. This assertion was capped by a roaring string of unpublishable expletives which must have shattered the still of the night for a distance of two blocks.

I wasn't accustomed to such language, especially from Bob, but it was gratifying to know that, apparently, he wasn't too badly hurt. Ann woke up, either from the gas explosion or from Bob's, and started to cry. Instead of going to the shed, I went into the bedroom to get her. By the time I picked her up, Bob was in the kitchen lounging nonchalantly against the ice box.

"Welcome to Anchor Inn," I told him. "We *hope* your stay . . ."

"That ironer is a little tricky," Bob said, using the half-whisper again. "I had a little trouble lighting the gas. I thought the newspaper had gone out, and when I came back and leaned over to see why the gas hadn't caught . . . By the way, did you happen to hear something that sounded a little like an explosion?"

"I heard two things that sounded like explosions," I replied.

"Two things?" Bob asked sheepishly.

"Two things," I nodded. "So did everyone else in the neighborhood. If I know Mrs. Macy, the pie wagon will be here any minute."

"Can we help it," my dignified co-proprietor replied innocently, "if some uncouth fellow, rushing the season, sets off a large fire-cracker practically in our back yard, and then bursts into profanity when the pyrotechnic burns his fingers?"

"If that's going to be your story," I suggested, "you'd better wash the soot off your face and change your clothes before the law arrives."

Ann went back to sleep without too much coaxing. I heard one of the guests close his bedroom door, come down the front stairs without tiptoeing, and then knock on our kitchen door. It was Mr. Jenkins, one of the recent bridegrooms, who proved to be one of the nicest and stupidest men of our acquaintance. His wife proved to be nice too, equally stupid, and—according to Bob—sensationally constructed. It may be said in Mr. Jenkins' favor that he believed in signs and was among the few guests who bothered to knock before entering the kitchen.

"You folks got some ice?" Mr. Jenkins asked.

"Sure," said Bob, using his normal voice. "I'll get it for you. I'm sorry about the lights going out a while back."

"Did they go out?" asked our young guest. "I guess," he blushed, "ours were *turned* out. We did hear some shouting out back, though."

"Shameful, wasn't it?" grinned Bob.

"I don't know," said Mr. Jenkins. "For a while we thought this place was a morgue. It gave us the creeps, know what I mean? We were sort of glad to hear some racket. Care to join us in a nightcap?"

"No thanks," I declined for Bob, "we're waiting for the police."

Since neither the law nor Mrs. Macy arrived, Bob finally deduced that, by some stroke of fortune, she had not been at home at the time of the explosion. I deduced something which I consider a good deal more probable—that she had heard everything, and

84

that Bob had her wrapped so tightly around his little finger, that she decided to make believe she hadn't heard anything.

It was good to be talking in a normal tone of voice again. As far as I was concerned, I agreed with young Mr. Jenkins. The morgue had given me the creeps, too.

6 ~ Belle and Bellhop

Although I'm not a particularly good cook, I didn't anticipate too much trouble in preparing breakfasts for our guests. I've always believed that breakfast in bed, while an uncomfortable and somewhat messy operation, is symbolic of the type of luxury that one likes to encounter on vacation. Consequently, we had decided to give our guests the option of being served in their rooms or of coming down and eating on the side porch, which had been converted into a dining room.

My firm agreement with Bob was that I'd fix the food and serve the guests in the dining room, and that he'd deliver the trays to the guests who wanted breakfast in bed.

But when it came time for Bob to assume his duties as a bellboy, he tried to welsh on the agreement.

"I don't like the idea of being a flunky," he told me while I was squeezing the oranges the next morning. "Let them come down here and eat."

"But we want them to come back next year, and we want them to tell their friends about the inn," I reasoned. "Go on, now. Keep your promise."

"And I'll feel like a fool, going into people's rooms when they're in bed and lounging around in nightgowns and all," he complained. "I won't know which way to look."

"Just pretend they're dressed. You'll get used to it. Find out what they want to eat, and whether they want to eat it up there or down here. And how about me? If I'm willing to be the chambermaid, you ought to be willing to be the bellboy."

"How about coming with me, just for this morning?" Bob urged. "You know, it might look friendly and nice if we both showed up to tell them about breakfast, a sort of husband and wife . . ."

"No," I said. "Get going."

Still complaining, Bob took a pad and pencil, and started up the stairs. He returned a few minutes later, and it was immediately apparent that he had not found the chore as unpleasant as he had expected.

"Wow," said Bob. "The Jenkinses say they'll be down in five minutes. Wow."

"Wow what?" I inquired.

"Wow Mrs. Jenkins," said Bob.

He explained that he had chosen their door to knock on first, since we had had the rather friendly conversation with Mr. Jenkins the night before.

"I thought I'd start out with someone I halfway knew," Bob explained, "and learn the ropes on them."

When Bob had knocked, the young husband—already dressed and still not accustomed to thinking in terms of a female roommate—had automatically answered, "Come in." As Bob entered,

Belle and Bellhop

Mrs. Jenkins was just starting to get into her clothes. She whooped, looked for a place to hide, couldn't immediately find one, grabbed a sheet off the bed, wrapped herself in it, and finally, since they didn't have a private bath, made a dash for the closet.

"And what did you do," I asked irritably, "stand there and gape at her?"

"I certainly did not," Bob assured me. "I did just as you said. I pretended she was dressed, and asked them what they'd have for breakfast."

"Oh, fine," I snapped. "And what are they going to have?"

Bob paused, looked blankly at the pad he was carrying, and found it empty.

"Just fix them scrambled eggs," he replied guiltily.

Lest there be a rush of males into the business of operating an inn, I should report that Bob has never yet quite duplicated his initial pleasant experience as a bellhop. In all fairness, though, I should perhaps add that I don't believe he has completely given up hope. Certainly that morning, he could hardly wait to get back upstairs and see what the other newlywed couple would have for breakfast.

Bob's initial experience in taking Miss Thomas' order was anything *but* pleasant. When he knocked on her door, she threw it open immediately and stood, hands-on-hips, glaring at him—a tall, angular, gloomy woman, ramrod straight, with black hair worn tightly plastered to her scalp. Miss Thomas, who felt it her Christian duty to call attention to laxness, wherever it might exist, now proceeded to do just that.

"I've been dressed for two hours, waiting for you," she said. "I like my breakfast promptly at six-thirty. I don't approve of people who loll around in bed all morning."

As Bob had been up since five o'clock, helping me get things straight downstairs, and as both of us had just about forgotten what it was to loll, he found it difficult to remain civil.

"I'm sorry," he finally managed, "but we don't start serving until eight-thirty."

"Unless I can get my breakfast at six-thirty," she threatened, "I'll have to move someplace else."

"We certainly wouldn't want you to stay here if you're not happy," Bob said.

Miss Thomas decided to change the subject. "Did you remember to take my egg out of the ice box last night?"

"What egg?" asked Bob, without stopping to think.

"I distinctly told your wife exactly how my breakfast egg is to be prepared."

"Oh, yes," Bob recalled belatedly.

"Did you remember to take it out of the ice box last night?"

"Perhaps my wife did," Bob stalled, although I think he was pretty sure I hadn't.

"We," said Miss Thomas, "shall see. If you'll be good enough to bring my breakfast up here, I'll eat now and then you can move me to another room."

"You're checking out?" Bob asked, almost hopefully.

"I'm going to try it here one more night, since I suppose you need the money," she replied magnanimously. "I assume that the lights don't fail *every* night. But of course I can't stay in a front room where the street light shines in my eyes. Incidentally, didn't I hear a baby crying last night?"

"You may have," said Bob, who hoped that Ann was all she had heard. "We have one."

"I thought so," exclaimed Miss Thomas, as if that were the final proof of our carelessness. "I'm allergic to babies."

"I certainly hope you never have any then," Bob observed agreeably. "We're crazy about ours."

Miss Thomas opened her mouth to reply, apparently decided she had better not pursue the subject, and settled for a look that was meant to wither.

"Do you have a dog?" she asked finally. "I can't stand dogs."

Bob admitted regretfully that we didn't own a dog.

"I could have sworn," she said suspiciously, "that I heard a dog howling in the back yard last night, not long after the lights came back on again and just before the baby started to cry. I certainly heard *something* howling. Are you sure you don't have a dog?"

"We plead guilty," sighed Bob, "to having a baby and innocent to having a dog. As I mentioned before, Miss Thomas, if you don't think you're going to be happy here . . ."

"If you would bring my breakfast," she interrupted, "I would be a sight happier."

Bob left, with the door practically slammed in his face. Of course I had forgotten all about taking her egg out of the ice box the night before. And of course, not being at that time familiar with her uncanny ability to tell how long an egg had been cooked, I confidently thought I could fool her by using a cold egg and boiling it for three and a half minutes.

It didn't fool her at all. When Bob returned upstairs with the tray, she noticed some minute cracks in the shell even before she opened it, and informed him:

"I will spare you the embarrassment of repeating what would be a falsehood, young man. This egg was not taken from the ice box last night, was it?"

"I thought," said Bob, deciding he might be able to jolly her along as he had Mrs. Macy, "that was the very falsehood you were going to spare me."

Miss Thomas gingerly opened the egg, and her pink nose twitched in revulsion.

"Ruined," she snapped. "If I had wanted something to take on a picnic, I would have ordered it. This egg has been boiled three and a half minutes if it has been boiled a second. Don't deny it."

"Amazing," smiled Bob, still trying to jolly her. "It was boiled exactly three and a half minutes, at nine feet above sea level. Now if we had been in the mountains, where water boils at a slightly lower temperature, I guess . . ."

"I am well aware of the elementary laws of physics, Mr. Gilbreth," she broke in. "The point is that we are *not* in the mountains. Are we?"

"Would you like my wife to boil you another egg?" Bob asked, still good-naturedly.

"I've lost my appetite," declared Miss Thomas.

Bob gave up. "So have I," he stated. "If you don't want your egg, just leave it on your plate. I'll give it to the dog."

"A minute ago," Miss Thomas said triumphantly, as if she were a district attorney who had just trapped a defendant into clumsily purjuring himself, "you just finished telling me you didn't have a dog. Don't deny it."

"It is quite true that we don't have a dog," Bob shouted, "yet!"

Bob stalked down stairs, and threw his order pad across the kitchen.

"I quit," he hollered at me. "Get yourself a new bellboy. I'm going to see a man about a dog."

"What's the matter," I couldn't resist asking, "was that other honeymoon gal fully dressed?"

"Save your efforts at humor for the customers," Bob urged.

Belle and Bellhop

"After this you can be the bellboy, and I'll hard-boil the three-minute eggs."

"But I thought, after you popped in on Mrs. Jenkins, that you *wanted* to be the bellboy," I teased him. "Don't deny . . ."

"The next person," said Bob, "who asks me not to deny something, is apt to get a punch in the nose, regardless of sex, age, race, creed, color or marital status."

Finally realizing that he was not in a particularly receptive mood for my witticisms, I listened patiently to his tale of woe.

"We've got to find a way to get rid of the old crab," he concluded. "That's all there is to it."

I hated to lose a customer, and also thought that perhaps I could handle her. But after moving her luggage to a west room, and whisking out the rug and wool blanket, and getting a taste of not denying that the west room was deliberately designed to focus the afternoon sun in her eyes when she was trying to take a nap, and then moving her to a back room which happened to be directly over our kitchen where she could hear every word we said, and again doing the whisking—after all of that, I was ready to agree with Bob that she had to go.

She was on my mind so much, by that time, it seems inconceivable I could have forgotten the next night about removing her egg. But I *did* forget. Although Bob tried to rectify the matter by dashing over to Mrs. Macy's to see if he could borrow a room-temperature egg, neither Mrs. Macy nor any of our immediate neighbors happened to have one. And so Bob had to go through another scene with Miss Thomas, at the climax of which he departed from her room whistling rudely for an imaginary Fido.

For the next few days, I managed to remember her egg, even though Anchor Inn was rapidly filling with guests and both Bob and I were so busy we were getting only a few hours interrupted sleep at night. Among the things which interrupted our sleep, incidentally, was the front doorbell. After answering it two or three times, and finding no one there, Bob sat up one night to try to catch the prankster. It turned out that the culprit, far from being a prankster, was Mr. Jenkins—the friendly but not too intellectual bridegroom. One of Bob's signs, under the front doorbell, said "Ring Bell for Manager." The sign was meant for persons seeking accommodations, but Mr. and Mrs. Jenkins interpreted it as a request to inform the manager that they were back on the premises after spending the evening up-town.

Even when I remembered Miss Thomas' egg, she seemed determined to make life miserable for us. Perhaps she wanted to discipline us for removing the source of the morning scenes which had given her so much pleasure. Two mornings in a row, when Bob delivered an egg cooked exactly to her specifications, she said she wasn't hungry and couldn't eat a thing.

Also, when she came out of the inn and saw Ann playing in the yard, she would clap a handkerchief to her twitching, allergic nose —even if Ann were a hundred feet away—and flee down the sidewalk. I don't know what the neighbors thought about this, but I know what it looked like. I resented the implication that I was such a careless mother Ann could not be tolerated even up wind at a distance of one hundred feet.

Whenever Ann cried at night, which wasn't very often until Miss Thomas' arrival, the spinster would pound on the ceiling with the heel of a shoe. This only served to make Ann howl all the louder.

The heel-pounding got so irritating that Bob and I were soon ready to go to any extreme to avoid it. Since we could neither get rid of Miss Thomas nor stop her from pounding, there was no alternative but to approach the problem from the opposite direction and work on Ann. Punishment of Ann was out of the question, because it would have resulted in a clamor that might have waked the entire inn. That left only bribery.

Consequently, every time Ann so much as whimpered during the night, I would leap out of bed and pick her up, and Bob would leap out of bed and start showering her with toys and food.

It required only a couple of nights of such treatment for Ann to realize that her life had changed miraculously for the better. All she had to do, to be both coddled and stuffed with goodies at any time of night, was simply to open her mouth and holler. She proceeded to do both, with nerve-racking regularity, while Miss Thomas' heel thumped out a spiteful accompaniment.

After some of Bob's family arrived at The Shoe, we started taking Ann over there and leaving her for the night, when she cried. But I'm afraid they spoiled her, too, and that she also treasured the excitement of precipitous departure from her bed and board. In any event, her crying spells became nightly affairs and continued, while the rafters rattled under Miss Thomas' promptings, until we got Ann out of the inn.

As I may have implied before, Bob's family is not exactly reticent in the matter of offering advice, whether or not solicited, to the youngest of the family's male members. They have been doing this ever since Bob was born, and the practice was a well-established part of Tradition by the time he had learned to walk. Since Tradition can no more be changed than tears can wash out words writ by the moving finger, Bob never had a chance to put up an argument—that anybody would listen to—against the practice.

All of the advice is well meaning, and some of it is even good. I thought the advice of one of Bob's brothers, in the matter of Miss Thomas, was generally sound.

"Obviously, you've got to get rid of the old girl," summarized the brother, after we had dropped off Ann one night and recounted our latest tale of heel-pounding. "Right?"

"Right," I said. "She's ruining Ann and demoralizing us."

"Maybe," said Bob, who had conditioned himself to listen to family advice, but to remain noncommittal about following it.

"Since she says she can't stand dogs," continued the brother, "you've got to get a dog."

"We've thought of that, of course," agreed Bob. "But we don't want a dog. It would disturb our other guests. Besides, we've written a lot of reservation letters telling people that they can't bring pets, and that we don't have any."

"But you can *borrow* a dog," pointed out Bob's brother. "Why don't you borrow Belle?"

Belle, the dog in question, at that moment was scratching herself lazily and shamelessly on a rug which bore a number of old stains attesting her lack of training in a matter considered basic for house pets. Through the years, most of the members of Bob's family had had a hand, at one time or another, in trying to train Belle. The results had been uniformly unsuccessful. Now seven or eight years old, Belle had recently been spared further training, when it was finally reluctantly concluded that it was impossible to teach an old dog a new trick, however basic.

The dog was greatly treasured, nonetheless, particularly since she was the offspring of what Bob kept assuring me was a thoroughbred collie. The collie had been a family retainer for years, prior to her demise before Bob left home for college. But if Belle's mother were a thoroughbred, nobody could have accused her of being a snob. Belle was actual, living proof that her mother had been extraordinarily democratic in her associations with dogs of the opposite sex.

Belle herself was as ugly, affectionate, stupid, massive, disrepu-

table, lackadaisical, uninhibited, odoriferous a mongrel as ever
dropped a litter of ill-begotten pups—which, incidentally, she per-
sisted in doing through the years on the least provocation.

"Are you sure," I asked Bob's brother sarcastically, "you could
spare her?"

"Well of course we wouldn't let just anybody borrow her," he
assured me, "but naturally you and Bob are different."

"I was afraid of that," I said. "No thanks. The idea of borrowing
a dog may be all right, but not Belle."

"Don't worry. She won't mind. I doubt if she'd know the difference between The Shoe and Anchor Inn."

I doubted it too, and especially that the dim-witted creature
would know the difference between our valuable old hooked rugs
and the one on which she was shedding hair and, probably, fleas.
But for once Bob decided the family advice had merit.

"You know, I'm beginning to like the idea," Bob said. "Look
at it this way, Barb. Even people who adore dogs can barely
tolerate Belle. Since Miss Thomas hates all dogs, can you imagine
what her reaction will be to Belle?"

Bob cackled in fiendish anticipation. I had to admit that he had
stated his argument most convincingly. I was beginning to get a
mental picture of the pony-sized Belle lumbering up to Miss
Thomas in our lobby, while the spinster tucked up her skirts and
tried to beat a nose-twitching retreat. I cackled, too.

"Come here, Belle," Bob ordered, snapping his fingers. "Come
here, girl." He snapped his fingers again. "Come here, you stupid
fleabag."

It finally penetrated Belle's dense brain that someone was calling
her, and that she was about to receive some attention. Other than
food, which she devoured in huge quantities, there was nothing
which Belle loved more than attention. She stretched thoroughly,

labored to her feet, hesitated while she meditated what obviously was a thorny problem, and studied the occupants of the room carefully. At last, deciding with typical acumen that I was the possessor of the masculine voice and snapping fingers, she came loping over to me.

Before I could hide or even brace myself, she put two heavy, unsanitary paws in my lap, almost upsetting the rocker in which I was sitting, and had the additional impudence to think she could lick my face. She thought right, too, because I couldn't push her away unless I wanted to go over backwards. It instantly became sickeningly clear that, among Belle's other liabilities, she possessed the oral ailment that even one's best friend hesitates to discuss.

"If somebody doesn't get her off of me," I threatened, trying to keep my lips closed because her tongue was sweeping impartially over my face, "I'll . . . I'll . . ."

"She's only trying to be friendly," Bob's brother assured me. "She won't hurt you."

"Get her off of me," I begged.

"She won't bite you, honey," said Bob.

"Just the same," I muttered, doing my best to swallow my lips while the dog slobbered, "get her off of me. Please!"

"Isn't it funny," said my brother-in-law, "how everybody's afraid of Belle? And she wouldn't hurt a flea."

"Too lazy," Bob nodded.

The discussion continued along this line for some time, before Bob finally decided that Belle was perhaps overdoing her affections, and pulled her away. In the interval, Belle apparently became convinced she had found someone who enjoyed her attentions. In any event, she continued to shower them upon me, whenever we subsequently met.

Bob and I went to get Belle the next morning, and she and I

had quite a moist reunion. She was all over me in our car, driving to Anchor Inn, and once we arrived there I learned the meaning of the phrase "dog your steps." She dogged mine, following me at her clumsy, loping, tail-wagging trot as I crossed and recrossed the kitchen gathering up the dishes. She looked so longingly at the left-over toast, eggs, and bacon that I didn't have the heart to deprive her of them. After that, she was my slave, but a lot of good it did me to have a slave that couldn't understand the simplest order and whose idea of being helpful consisted of trying to put her paws on my shoulders so she could wash my face.

When I went up to start my chambermaid duties, I left Belle secure in the kitchen, while Bob departed to do some laundry. Someone must have opened the kitchen door, however, because within a few minutes I heard something that sounded like a horse stumbling upstairs. Before I could straighten up from the bed I was making, she discovered me and rushed at me with such enthusiasm that she toppled me over.

After a brief wrestling match on the bed, in which Belle won the first two falls, she finally became winded and decided to rest in a neutral corner, where her tail thumped the floor in ecstasy. It was obvious that, in Belle's studied opinion, the shift from The Shoe—where she was generally ignored and fed only at supper time; to Anchor Inn—where she had a playmate and received an extra meal for breakfast—was dog heaven. She yawned hideously and stretched her grotesque body in lazy contentment. Belle had never had it so good.

Since the occupants of the room had gone to the beach for the morning, I decided to let her stay there with me until I finished making the beds. Perhaps, in spite of myself, I was growing fond of her.

I left the room momentarily to get a couple of clean pillow cases.

I guess Belle started to follow me, and lost me when I went into the linen closet.

At any rate, Miss Thomas picked that precise time to emerge from a bathroom into the hall. She didn't see Belle, but Belle followed her instead of me.

Admittedly, we had brought Belle to Anchor Inn to drive away Miss Thomas but we honestly hadn't intended to scare her.

That lady was fully dressed and was returning to her bedroom to pick up her pocketbook, before taking her morning stroll. The pocketbook happened to be on her bed. When Miss Thomas leaned over to pick it up, Belle must have decided that Miss Thomas was I, and that it was time for us to have another wrestling match.

I am only speculating about all of this, of course, because no one can say for sure what goes on inside a dog's head, especially a dog like Belle. It seems insultingly improbable to me that any living creature with eyes in its head could have mistaken a back view of Miss Thomas for a back view of me, but I can find no other satisfactory explanation for what followed. This much I do know for a fact:

Belle charged enthusiastically at Miss Thomas' angular and protruding rear, toppled her over onto the bed, and climbed up there with her.

The first clue I had of any of this was a bloodcurdling scream of pure terror, which scared me so that for a moment I couldn't make my legs move. When I got control of myself and rushed back into the hall, I saw a yellow streak which was Belle, emerging from Miss Thomas' room and disappearing down the stairs in two prodigious, house-shaking leaps. If I hadn't seen it with my own eyes, I would have taken an oath that Belle couldn't have moved even half that fast.

And then screams came again and again from poor Miss

Thomas. When I reached her room, she was curled up on the top of her dresser, trying to make herself as small as possible. I never have been able to figure out how she got there, unless she leaped directly from the bed, which was a good six feet away. However it was accomplished, it must have been quite a sight.

Bob heard the screams and came running. So did the elderly married couple, who still weren't speaking to each other. Fortunately, they happened to be the only other guests in the inn at the time.

So too did Mrs. Macy—after calling the police to assist us with what she was sure must be a maniac.

By the time Mrs. Macy arrived, Miss Thomas had stopped her screaming and was in hysterics. Bob and I had managed to get her off the dresser and onto her bed, where she was shivering and chattering incoherently.

Never losing her dignity, Mrs. Macy immediately took charge. She knelt beside the bed and talked firmly and competently in her half-whisper to Miss Thomas.

"Get hold of yourself, woman!" she ordered. "You are making a disgraceful spectacle of yourself."

Miss Thomas paid no attention.

"Get hold of yourself, I say!" demanded Mrs. Macy. Suddenly she struck Miss Thomas quite sharply across the face.

There had been many times during the last few days when I would have given a great deal to do exactly that myself, only with a closed fist instead of an open hand. Now I felt so guilty that the slap brought tears of pain to my eyes.

But it had the desired effect on Miss Thomas. The hysterics stopped, and she quickly pulled herself together. She arose slowly from the bed, as Mrs. Macy got up from her knees. The two faced each other. As dignified as was Mrs. Macy, Miss Thomas matched her pressed lip for pressed lip, and aloof eyebrow for aloof eyebrow.

"Was that necessary, madam?" inquired Miss Thomas.

"It is the prescribed treatment, I believe," replied Mrs. Macy.

"Then, I thank you," said Miss Thomas. "And I would consider it a favor"—she swept all of us with a withering glance—"if my room could be cleared of perfect strangers and curiosity seekers."

We all started to leave, but Miss Thomas decided she wanted to set the record straight before any of us started false rumors.

"One moment," she said. "I am not in the habit of causing disturbances. I am also unaccustomed to being attacked by large animals."

Bob, who still didn't know that the dog had been upstairs, and Mrs. Macy exchanged significant glances. The elderly couple edged out of the door and departed hastily.

"There, there," said Mrs. Macy, now convinced that the best policy would be to humor her until the police could send for a straight-jacket. "You just relax now, and we'll stand right outside the door and make sure that no more animals come in."

"But I tell you, I *was* attacked by a large, fur-bearing animal."

"Of course you were," Mrs. Macy soothed her.

"The island is alive with them," put in Bob.

"Could it have been a dog?" I asked guiltily, more to tip off Bob than to find out whether Miss Thomas had got a good look at Belle.

"There, there," said Mrs. Macy.

"I don't think it was a dog," Miss Thomas shook her head. "If it was a dog, it would have had to be a huge one."

I could see Bob, first grasping the situation and then looking furtively around the room to see whether Belle had shed any hair. Apparently she hadn't. Then Bob disappeared silently, and

I guessed correctly that he had gone downstairs to make sure that Belle had departed from the premises. A few moments later, I could hear him assuring two policemen that their assistance, however appreciated, was no longer needed.

Mrs. Macy, still determined to be helpful, decided that in spite of Bob's dismissing the police it would be best to try to get rid of Miss Thomas for us then and there.

"I shouldn't think," she said in her reasonable half-whisper, "you would want to remain in an inn where large fur-bearing animals stalk the corridors. I think you would be much happier in a hotel, don't you?"

"Your thoughts on the matter," replied Miss Thomas, "are of great interest, I am sure. Since you obviously think I am a mental case, I am going to leave the matter up to Mrs. Gilbreth." She turned to me and although she was as overbearing as ever, there was something pathetic about her, too. "Do you believe," she asked me, "that a large animal was in this room?"

I still wanted to get rid of her, but not enough to make her doubt her own sanity.

"I believe you," I said. "I do think, though, that you'd be happier someplace else, don't you?"

"I'd be happier if you both get out of here," replied Miss Thomas, true to form. "The more I think of it, the more I think it must have been a large dog."

"I'm sure that's what it was," I confessed.

"Is it apt to happen again?" she demanded suspiciously.

The time seemed ripe for a showdown. "It is not apt to happen again," I said, "if there are no more floor-knockings when my baby cries."

"I'm not sure I understand this," said Mrs. Macy. "What's this about . . ."

"I'll explain later," I said wearily. "It's a long story."

I suppose that if I had begged Miss Thomas to stay, she would have left immediately. Since both Mrs. Macy and I had practically invited her to leave, she was determined to stay.

"I must say," she stated as she practically pushed us out of the room, "that when I wrote for reservations at what I had been told was a respectable quiet establishment, I had not reckoned with squalling children, vicious animals, *and* brawling, face-slapping neighbors."

Mrs. Macy is one of the most perfect ladies I have ever met, but for once she forgot herself.

"Another remark like that," she hollered, "and blow me down if you won't get your face slapped again."

"And one more heel-pounding on the floor when my baby cries," I said, utilizing effectively the half-whisper that Mrs. Macy had for the moment abandoned, "and I will call the police." Miss Thomas slammed her door, and Mrs. Macy put her hands on my shoulders as we marched single-file down the narrow front stairs, in a self-satisfied tandem. Bob was waiting for us in the lobby—with his mouth open.

7 ~ No Secrets from a Chambermaid

"Running a summer inn," Mrs. Macy once told me, "is like a merry-go-round that someone pushes you on in June, and you can't get off until September. Except that it isn't very merry."

Not very merry, perhaps, but usually interesting and sometimes down-right fascinating.

By mid-summer, Anchor Inn was full almost every night, and we had reservations booked pretty solidly until Labor Day. Sometimes Bob and sometimes I checked the guests in and out, so it was difficult for either of us to know at any given time what all of our guests looked like.

Late one morning, when Bob and I were talking in the lobby, a handsome, gray-haired man descended from the second floor, nodded pleasantly, and walked out into the street. I assumed that Bob had checked him in the night before, and Bob assumed that I had done so. It turned out that neither of us had. Since I had just finished cleaning the rooms upstairs, I knew he hadn't been visiting any of our guests. We never did find out where he came from, but nothing was missing from any of the rooms. Perhaps he had stayed at Anchor Inn in some previous year, knew the location of the facilities, and had simply dropped in to use a bathroom.

I got to know a good bit, though, about guests who stayed with us for a week or more. For some reason, people love to confide their secrets to chambermaids. And chambermaids, unless they are blind, often blunder on other secrets which people haven't intended to confide.

One middle-aged couple, for instance, informed me happily that, after years of failure, she was finally expecting a baby. She seldom left her room, because both of them were afraid that somehow she might lose the baby. And I never saw two people more thrilled about a forthcoming birth. When they'd talk about it, and tell me how they had been dreaming about it and hoping for it, they'd both glow. A secret they didn't tell me was that, during the whole two weeks they were with us, they had their dog with them in their room.

I never saw the animal, but on the second day I cleaned their room I thought I heard a muted bark. When the bark wasn't repeated, I dismissed the incident. I probably never would have thought about it again, but the day before they left I found an unmistakable sign that a dog had been under their bed. I cleaned up the sign, and didn't tell them about my discovery—since they were leaving. Besides, any dog so well behaved he could avoid detection by a chambermaid for thirteen days had earned the right to stay with his masters. I made it a point to check them out myself, when they finally left us, and didn't see the dog. I'd be willing to bet, though, that when their baby finally arrived and the dog was no longer an "only child," the poor little animal needed psychiatric treatment.

A chambermaid, even if she isn't especially inquisitive, can't help making appraisals of the financial status, intellectual attainments, love life, drinking habits, and personal foibles of the occupants of the rooms she cleans.

Many vacationers carry expensive-looking luggage, and know how to wear their clothes well. But labels on their suits and dresses, and the quality of their underthings usually give a more accurate financial picture. I hope no one gets the idea from any of this that I went poking into closets to examine labels or prying into dresser drawers to examine underthings—because I didn't. Fortunately or unfortunately, it is my nature to notice things. If a suit is slung over a chair with the label showing, I notice the label. The same goes for the quality of underthings left hanging in a bathroom.

Wastebaskets are a well of information as to the habits of guests. Again, I don't want to give the impression that I pumped the well to the extent of piecing together personal letters and examining every empty bottle of hair dye. But it is bound to make an impression on a chambermaid—or at any rate on *this* chambermaid —if an empty fifth of gin is rattling around by itself every morning in the wastebasket of a sweet young thing in whose mouth butter would not melt. And well-thumbed copies of movie and confession magazines, in the wastebasket of a dean of women from a New England institution of higher learning, do not indicate a taste for Euripedes as light summer reading.

To tell the truth, I *did* paw through the wastebaskets insofar as magazines were concerned, because I saw no reason to throw them out until Bob and I had a chance to read them. That went for the movie and confession magazines, too.

I feel I ought to assure not only our past guests but the guests to whom we hope to cater in the future that the very large majority of our clientele is friendly, considerate, and normal. Every inn, however, has its exceptions; they are the ones who make the best stories.

Later that summer, for instance, we had a male guest in his fifties who was nondescript except for a pair of heavy-lense glasses which magnified his eyes so much that you could never see all of them at the same time. He arrived alone, although his reservation letter had requested twin beds.

"I never sleep two consecutive nights in the same bed," he explained. "Germs." ·

"Germs?" I inquired.

"B. T. Germs," he said, as if he were introducing somebody to us. "The 'B. T.' is for body temperature. They die in twenty-four hours if they're not kept at body temperature, and after they're dead you don't have to worry about them. But if you sleep in the same bed every night, they not only stay alive, they multiply."

"If you have B. T. Germs," I told him, fearing some sort of an epidemic, "I'm not sure you ought to stay with us."

"Everybody has them," he smiled at my ignorance. "But not everybody knows what to do about them. That's why I like a bed to be really *aired*. Of course I'll pay the double rate, for using two beds."

"It must make it expensive whenever you're away from home," Bob said.

"Not when you figure what I save in doctors' bills. I haven't paid a doctor's bill in seventeen years. Did anybody sleep last night in the room I'm going to occupy?"

"I'm afraid so," I admitted.

"In both beds?"

"I'm afraid so," I repeated. "Every bed we had was full last night."

"There's no need to apologize," he smiled again. "I'm accustomed to it. I find that I usually have to sit up all night, when I start a vacation."

I showed him to his room, and first thing he did was to rip both beds apart.

"They'll be dead as doornails in another eighteen hours," he told me with some satisfaction.

Then he got out an atomizer, and after I closed the door behind me I could hear him spraying the room.

He sat up all that first night. During the remainder of the week he was with us, he slept first in one twin bed and then in the other.

He wasn't afraid of germs on the breakfasts which Bob brought him because, as he explained, food wasn't at body temperature. But Bob and I both went around with our bodies at body temperature, and additionally didn't observe the rudimentary B. T. law of sleeping in alternate beds. So our guest always atomized his room after I cleaned it and after Bob arrived with breakfast.

At the end of the week, he disappeared with his luggage and without paying his bill. Luckily, I discovered his absence before the afternoon steamer sailed, and Bob hurried down to the dock to see if he could locate him.

Bob found him there, and patiently explained that we were not running an eleemosynary institution, even for those guests who were considerate enough to give us free hygienic advice and to leave their rooms practically free of B. T. germs.

"You said you hadn't paid a doctor's bill in seventeen years," Bob added. "How long since you have paid a hotel bill?"

"You mean you want the cash *right now?*" asked the germ man, as if Bob had made a ridiculous request.

"Well, it's certainly customary," Bob pointed out.

"How about a check, instead?"

"Do you have a checkbook with you?"

"Right here in my inside pocket."

"Too close to body temperature," Bob decided. "Cash. At the double-room rate. That's fifty-five dollars."

"But my cash is at B. T., too!"

"Just fork it over," Bob demanded. "Occasionally, I don't mind living dangerously."

The guest extracted six ten dollar bills from his wallet and gave them to Bob, but he wouldn't accept five dollars in change.

"*You* can live dangerously if you want to," he told Bob, "but don't expect *me* to. Mail me a check—you've got my address."

Another of our male guests collected stones—not unusual varieties, as far as I could see, but the rounder the better.

We didn't particularly object at first, because by then we were fairly accustomed to collectors. Rocks at least do not smell or attract flies, as do the starfish and horseshoe crabs which some of our guests accumulate. Also, we had found that few people can visit the seashore without yielding to the temptation of trying to strip the beaches of shells.

But the rocks intrigued me. First they covered the top of his dresser, over which he had considerately spread a bathtowel—either to protect the dresser or the rocks from damage; I never could decide which.

Then they overflowed onto his desk and finally—toward the end of the ten days for which he had reservations—they covered a good portion of the floor. It was almost impossible to vacuum without coming a cropper, and when I mentioned that fact to him he suggested that I forego any cleaning at all. Again, I couldn't decide whether this was out of consideration for me or because he was afraid I'd bruise the rocks.

When the time came for the collector to check out, Bob went up to help with the bags. Since the man apparently had made no provision to pack his rocks, Bob decided to approach obliquely the subject of what we were supposed to do with them.

"I've heard of people who didn't leave a stone unturned," Bob said politely. "I think you're the first person I ever met who first turned them all, and then brought them home."

"Indeed?" inquired our guest, also politely.

"Well," said Bob, deciding he might as well ask the question directly, "aren't you going to take them with you?"

"My dear fellow," said the collector, exactly as if Bob were trying to pawn something off on him, "what in the world would I want with a lot of useless rocks?"

"A good question," Bob conceded. "And am I supposed to tote those things out of here and throw them away?"

"Well, I would say, sir, that that's entirely up to you," our guest said.

Bob, who didn't relish the chore of wrestling with the rocks and who probably realized I would consider their removal not part of a chambermaid's duties, can seldom resist an untactful remark when getting rid of such a guest.

"Next year," he suggested while carefully picking a path among the rocks, "why don't you spend your vacation at Plymouth?" He leaned over and whispered conspirator-fashion in the guest's ear. "They have a *great big* one there."

Toward the end of that first summer, when we happened to have several rooms vacant, two good-looking post-debutantes from New

York rang the doorbell and asked about our prices. When we told them, they seemed utterly shocked.

"We certainly can't afford anything like *that*," one of them said. "We're on a very limited budget. Don't you have anything less expensive?"

We did have a few rooms on the third floor, which we had used as overflow accommodations and at reduced rates, during the peak of the season. There was nothing particularly the matter with these rooms, except that we hadn't had a chance to decorate them properly. We told the two girls that they could have a third-floor room for two dollars each a night.

After examining the room, they said they thought a dollar and a half apiece would be a fairer price.

I had made it a policy not to be bargained down on our rates, and told them so. This brought forth a heart-rending tale of how they had saved their money so that they could return to Nantucket, scene of many happy childhood memories when their families had been affluent; and of how much they had both looked forward to this brief vacation as an interlude in two colorless lives of near poverty.

Bob, having heard the tale, was prepared to offer the room for nothing. However, since I had noticed their tailored suits, airplane luggage, expensive spectator shoes and alligator purses, I let them know that while their autobiographies moved me deeply the price was still two dollars apiece per night.

"I guess we can afford the rate for one night," the spokesman for the pair finally decided. "But tomorrow we'll have to look for something less expensive."

Bob looked at me as if I were Scrooge, but I still knew that the cost of the clothes they were wearing would have paid a year's mortgage interest on Anchor Inn.

"You see," the spokesman continued plaintively, screwing up her mouth little girl fashion and batting her eyelashes at Bob, "we had dreamed of spending a whole, wonderful week on Nantucket. But of course if we are forced to pay exorbitant rates, we'll have to go home before that."

"She doesn't mean," said the second girl, also batting her eyelashes at Bob, "that your rates would be exorbitant to most people. It's just that they seem that way to *us,* because we're not used to resort prices."

"If you had a room that wasn't quite so desirable," nodded the spokesman, "it would do us perfectly well. Our needs are simple and . . ."

"The only room that isn't quite so desirable," I cut her off, "is the one we sleep in."

I wanted to add that we could perhaps set up a pup tent for them in the back yard, at fifty cents apiece; but Bob was now looking at me as if I had kicked the crutches out from under Tiny Tim, and I decided I had gone far enough.

They spent the night. The following day they looked for something less expensive. Apparently they didn't find it, because when they returned they told us they guessed they could scrape up the money to stay with us for a few more days.

Actually, they stayed with us for three weeks, quickly got into the social whirl, joined the Beach Club and the Yacht Club, rented a car for the duration of their stay, and one day left the car unused while they additionally rented a jeep to drive around on the beaches.

But Bob remained more or less on their side until the day they asked to borrow the phone to call a boat-renting concern. The kitchen door was open, and while the second girl giggled into her handkerchief and had the effrontery to wink at us, the spokesman pulled on the boat-renter the same line she had tried to pull on me.

"A hundred dollars!" the spokesman groaned into the telephone. "Oh, dear, of course that's out of the question. You see, we don't want anything like the *Queen Mary*. It's just that we owe so many social obligations that we thought we'd like to take some friends out for a day of tuna-fishing on a little cruiser."

This went on for some time, and when she finally hung up she announced jubilantly to her friend, "he came down to seventy dollars."

"Dirt cheap," the friend agreed.

After that, whenever Bob brought them their breakfast, he would inform them that if they found bacon and eggs too much of a strain on their budget, we could give them a better price on gruel.

8~ Death and the Umpire

Among the worries of an inn-keeper is the possibility that a guest
will become seriously or fatally ill. A seriously ill guest, especially
if the disease is contagious, is as welcome at an inn as any other
kind of plague. The same can be said, in spades, for a guest who
has the bad fortune to pass away on the premises.

I don't want to sound callous, but it should be apparent that
neither sickness nor death is good for business. I can think of
nothing which adds less to the gay holiday atmosphere of a
hostelry than a dead guest up in one of the bedrooms. Unless it is
two or more dead guests.

No one has died at Anchor Inn under our management, but
there have been a couple of occasions when we have had to track
down on the relatives of ill guests. It can be a frustrating job,
particularly if telephone circuits from Nantucket to the mainland

are busy, and if the relatives themselves have departed on vacations.

You can't very well ask incoming guests for information as to whom you should notify if they should have the tough luck to drop dead. Many guests—especially those whose age or appearance indicated the information might prove useful—would resent such an inquiry. But every inn-owner would sleep better at night if this information were in his files.

I know one inn-proprietor on Nantucket who has been through the experience of handling a dead guest. She says that, if she had it to do over again, she'd gladly trade places with the corpse.

She was cleaning her upstairs rooms, when she was somewhat demoralized by finding a dead guest lying on the floor of his bedroom. A doctor, who was hastily summoned, said death was due to a heart attack. She traced the next-of-kin to their home in Baltimore, only to find the entire household was fishing in Canada, miles from a telephone. By the time she finally found out what they wanted done with the remains, she was *completely* demoralized. And half of her guests had moved out.

The half which loyally remained passed along to new guests the word about the grim reaper's visit.

As might be expected, the story got distorted in the telling. The condition of the proprietor's nervous system was not improved when one new guest told her he wanted to be sure she didn't put him in the room "Where you found that couple hanging in the closet."

The upshot was that she couldn't rent the room again for the rest of that summer. And some of her regular guests still won't stay in that room, even though the incident happened four or five years ago.

When I asked her why she didn't move into the dead man's

room, and rent out her own bedroom, she looked at me as if she questioned my sanity.

"Who, me?" she gasped. "You mean sleep in there with the light out? I don't believe in ghosts, but not *me*."

I don't believe in ghosts either, but I know just how she felt.

We had a number of guests that first summer who were not very spry, and several who required a doctor's attention. But we had only one who I thought might die. And she was so pretty that I would have been inclined to forgive her for the inconvenience.

Her name was Mrs. Tatum, and she was about fifty-five, I would guess. She was a delicate-featured, fragile little thing, and you could tell that she had once been quite a beauty. Her husband, whom she called Tate, was about ten years older and worshiped her. He was a gruff, hearty sort of a man, but gentle and quiet spoken where she was concerned.

Mrs. Tatum complained of shortness of breath when they arrived, and I helped her into bed. Mr. Tatum came down into the kitchen a few minutes later to fill an ice pack for her. He explained that she had been in poor health for a long time, and that he had retired from business a couple of years before so that he could look out for her. It was important for her to have a mild climate, he said, so they spent the summers in New England and the winters in Florida. They didn't have any children.

They stayed with us for a month, and Mrs. Tatum seemed to feel worse every day. Migraine headaches kept her awake at night, her husband reported, and aspirin didn't do the headaches any good. What worried me most was that she didn't seem to have the *will* to get better.

But Mr. Tatum had enough will for both of them, in that regard. He'd hurry down to the drug store two or three times a day—and often in the middle of the night—to get medicines. He'd rub her back with lavender water, bring her lunch and dinner from a nearby restaurant, and read to her by the hour.

Sometimes she felt strong enough to sit in a rocker by her bedroom window, but too much sitting up caused her to clutch her side in pain, and Mr. Tatum would gently lift her back to bed.

I thought she was one of the bravest women I'd ever met. Only occasionally did she complain, although her face was usually screwed up in pain. And not more than once or twice did I hear a muffled groan escape her lips.

Bob and I became fond of both of them, and we honestly didn't mind on those occasions when Mr. Tatum would wake us to get ice, or borrow medicine, or seek advice about telephoning a doctor.

Still, I must admit that we breathed a sigh of relief when they finally checked out. Bob and Mr. Tatum carried her to a waiting taxicab, and I tucked blankets around her.

"Bless you both," she whispered to Bob and me.

I had to blink back tears. Mr. Tatum kissed me on the forehead, and hugged Bob tightly around the shoulders. We were distressed to hear, a few months later, that Mr. Tatum had passed away. Mrs. Tatum waited a decent interval before remarrying.

Our two oldest guests were anything but sickly, so we never had to worry about their health. They were both widows, eighty or older, who had been close friends ever since they were girls. When their husbands had died a number of years before, Miss Helen and Miss Lou had moved into the same house in Boston. They always took their vacations together, and it actually was an ideal arrangement for both of them—although neither would have admitted it under torture.

When I showed them their room, they both immediately de

cided that they wanted the same bed, which happened to be to the left of the night table and afforded the best reading light from the lamp on it. Each accused the other of being selfish, senile, and pigheaded for refusing to take the bed to the right of the night table.

"I declare, Lou," snapped Miss Helen, "you get to be more of a trial every day, always wanting your own way as you go into your second childhood."

"Second childhood!" bristled Miss Lou. "I'd like to know how you'd make out, if it wasn't for me. The way you're failing, I expect your son would put you away some place, except he knows I'll take care of you."

"Listen to her," Miss Helen urged me. "Do you know what she did at New Bedford? Gracious sake!"

"Now, ladies," I pleaded. "Let's settle this business about the beds."

"Lord, lord," scoffed Miss Lou. " 'Twasn't New Bedford. We didn't even go *near* New Bedford. It was Woods Hole. And, besides, it was a perfectly natural mistake to make."

"Woods Hole, then," conceded Miss Helen. "We *used* to go through New Bedford when we came to Nantucket, and that's how I got mixed up."

"See what I mean?' Miss Lou asked me. "She's failed so she doesn't even know how she got here."

"I know *exactly* how I got here," said Miss Helen. "And I know *exactly* what you did at Woods Hole. You picked up a suitcase that wasn't yours and started up the gangplank with it." Miss Helen leaned over and stage-whispered in my ear: "She's getting blind as a bat, poor thing."

"Well, at least I picked the suitcase up by mistake," said Miss Lou. "I didn't try to steal it, as some people I know might have done." Miss Lou mumbled something that was entirely unintelligible even to me.

"What's that?" demanded Miss Helen, cupping her ear. "Speak up, Lou."

"She's getting deaf as a post, poor woman," Miss Lou informed me.

I finally settled the dispute about who would sleep where, by bringing another night table and lamp from an unoccupied room. Miss Lou said she'd sleep next to the new night table in the less desirable bed—although actually the beds were identical. And Miss Helen said she'd take the best bed, regardless of which night table it was near. Then I had to go through some more umpiring, switching bureau scarves, because they had different crocheted edges, before they could decide who would take which dresser.

These two Solomon-like compromises on my part established me as the official mediator of their future disputes. These fusses ranged from who was cheating at double solitaire to whose dress was ironed the more skillfully to who was hogging the lion's share of their nightly bottle of wine.

Since their principal enjoyment in life came from winning arguments with each other, both spent a great deal of time trying to influence the umpire. They'd buttonhole me separately to tell me unlikely stories about the other's senility. And each sought to curry favor by helping me do my chores. My decisions came to be accepted as final—although not without audible complaints from the lady who happened to lose the verdict, and not without implications that I must be on the winner's payroll.

Miss Helen was always up first in the morning, and got in the habit of coming into the kitchen to assist me with the breakfast dishes. She wouldn't eat breakfast herself until Miss Lou got up, though, because many of their choicest arguments were reserved for the breakfast table. Bob enjoyed the arguments so much that he, too, got in the habit of deferring his breakfast until Miss Lou arrived, and then he'd sit down and eat with them. They liked to have an audience, of course.

"Poor Lou," Miss Helen sighed one morning as she washed dishes with thoroughness and surprising vigor. "You can always tell when a woman's failing. The first sign is that she wants to stay abed all morning. But then, she's much older than I. I'm more like a daughter to her than a friend."

"I think you're both amazingly vigorous," I said.

"Can I help you make the beds this morning, Barbara?" she asked eagerly.

"If you'll be nice to Miss Lou," I promised.

"Nice to her! If it wasn't for me, she wouldn't have a penny!"

"Doesn't she have an income of her own?"

"She has an income, but she wants to give it all to the church, poor soul. I keep telling her that at her age it's pretty late to start trying to buy her way into heaven."

"Is she religious?"

"Lord, no. Not really. But sometimes she reads the Bible like she was cramming for her finals. I have to sit next to her in church and take out some of the money she puts in the collection plate—and then slip it back in her pocketbook when she isn't looking. She's failed so she doesn't know what I'm doing. But I tell you, Barbara, it's a trial!"

Miss Lou had a different version when she found me alone that same afternoon. I was in the kitchen mending sheets, and Miss Lou pulled up a chair, to give me a hand. She threaded a needle on the first attempt, without aid of glasses, and proceeded to sew both better and faster than I.

"Poor Helen," she shook her head. "She used to be such a fine woman. I wish you could have known her, Barbara, before she reached her present condition of foolish second childhood. I guess you've noticed, haven't you, that she's a good deal older than I?"

"Where's Miss Helen now?" I dodged the question.

"She's taking an afternoon nap, poor soul. That's a sure sign that a woman's failing. She's lost all interest in how she looks. You've seen how her dresses look after she's ironed them."

"I think you both always look very nice," I temporized.

"I do what I can to spruce her up," Miss Lou nodded. "You know what she told me this morning?" Miss Lou laughed depreciatingly, to indicate that whatever insanities Miss Helen might have told me were of no consequence. But she carefully watched my reactions, just the same. "She told me you said she made beds better than I."

"You're both about the best bed-makers I ever saw," I smiled. "But I don't want you to think you have to help me with my work. Why don't you both just rest and have a good time."

"How can I rest and have a good time with the responsibility of looking out for Helen?" Miss Lou moaned. "I don't know how she'd get along without me. But it's humiliating to go to church with her."

"Oh, I can't believe that!"

"It's a terrible thing to tell, but she steals from the collection plate! And I've caught her going through my pocketbook!" Miss Lou put more thread in her needle, bit off the end expertly with her well-preserved teeth, and tied a knot without even having to look at what she was doing. "I haven't said anything to her about it, because I don't want to hurt her feelings. But it's a real cross to bear, living with a woman who is so far in her second childhood that she's started to steal."

It goes without saying that their arguments with each other

and the improbable tales which they bore to me were part of a defense mechanism. I think the two ladies were so fond of each other they were trying to convince themselves they could go it alone. Then, when death would inevitably separate them, the one left behind wouldn't be unprepared. They were marvelous company for me, and extremely helpful. Bob and I always enjoyed them, especially at breakfast.

Both had good appetites, and used the relative size of the portions which I served them as a yardstick of how they rated in my favor. The morning conversation usually got under way with a discussion of the napkins.

"I," Miss Helen would gloat, "got a nice, pink napkin for breakfast. Thank you, Barbara, for picking it out for me."

"Look how nice Bob ironed the green one for me," Miss Lou would reply. "Barbara gave me more orange juice than she did *you*. Thank you, Barbara."

"You didn't either, did you Barbara?" Miss Helen would ask. "Poor Lou," she'd stage whisper to Bob, "she can't even see who's got the most orange juice. Blind as a bat."

"Deaf as a doorpost, poor creature," Miss Lou would say. "How she can eat anything this morning after drinking practically a whole bottle of wine last night is beyond me. Tipsy as a sailor, she was."

Then Miss Lou would snatch her pocketbook and make quite a show of putting it beyond Miss Helen's reach. Noting this, Miss Helen would smile patiently, catch my eye, and turn her eyeballs heavenward in mute supplication. Miss Lou would retaliate by stage-whispering, "See what I mean?" Then she'd point her forefinger at her temple and cause the forefinger to describe small circles in the air.

If I had allowed it, Miss Lou and Miss Helen would have done most of my chores. They didn't enjoy the beach and quickly grew tired of strolling around town. But they seemed to adore working with me, and both were excellent housekeepers.

I let them help for an hour or so each day, and shooed them back to their room when I thought they might over-exert themselves. But, even so, I sometimes felt as if I were violating the child-labor laws.

9 ~ Skinning Cats

As at most resorts, the utility rates at Nantucket are designed to make certain that the seasonal householder pays what is euphemistically known as a "fair share" of the total cost of service.

Water charges, for instance, are figured not on how much water you use but on how many faucets, showers, and toilets you have in your house. And if your establishment is used for only four months, you still have to pay nine-tenths of the yearly rate.

Seasonal residences also are assessed a "special summer service rate" for electricity and gas. This is almost double the year-round rate.

The telephone company gets into the act, with a provision that if it connects your phone at all—even for one day—you must pay in advance for six months of service. Of course this means that many summer people, who actually use their phones for only a month or two, still must pay for half a year. Additionally, if they

want to be sure they have the same telephone number the following summer, they must get "temporary disconnection service" for
the winter.

I am not criticizing any of this, because I realize that a considerable capital investment is involved in bringing the utilities
to the summer homes. The investors naturally expect a fair return
on their money, and the equipment must be maintained on a
year-round basis whether or not the homes are occupied.

The only reason I am mentioning the situation at all is that
Anchor Inn, being a seasonal establishment, had to pay the high
rates. These rates are one of several factors which explain why
the running of a resort inn on Nantucket is not the gold mine that
many people imagine.

Those Nantucketers who had never operated an inn seemed to
be unanimous in the belief that Bob and I had amassed a tidy
fortune during that first summer. The grapevine, which pays avid
attention to all local financial news, carried the entirely accurate
report that Anchor Inn had had a full house almost every night
from the middle of July through Labor Day.

The Nantucketers were much too polite to come right out and
tell us in so many words that they suspected we were loaded, but
as we prepared to close the inn for the winter we received a
number of business callers who certainly conveyed that impression.

The consensus seemed to be that Bob, Ann, and I would be
headed for Florida, where, instead of running an inn, we would
enjoy the luxuries of a resort hotel for the next six or seven
months. The automobile dealers who came to call pointed out
that our fairly old sedan probably would give us a lot of trouble
on the long trip south, and certainly would disgrace us if we left
it parked in front of one of those swanky Florida hotels. The
dress-shoppe ladies, who were themselves preparing to close for

the winter, said that, of course, I would need an entirely new wardrobe. A man who operated a small travel agency suggested to Bob, that, rather than Florida, we might enjoy a Caribbean cruise. And practically every life-insurance man on the island expressed the knowing opinion that the time was ripe for Bob to take out adequate protection for his little family.

Totaling up our books at the end of the first season, we found that our profit, after we had met all the bills and taken care of the mortgage payments for the year, amounted to about fifteen hundred dollars.

If it can be argued that we were increasing our equity in the inn, and that an additional fifteen hundred dollars isn't too bad a profit for four months' work, it can also be argued that fifteen hundred dollars isn't a very handsome sum to support a family for the remaining eight months. Certainly there would be no trips to Florida and hardly any Caribbean cruises.

Also, it should be borne in mind that, especially when Anchor Inn was full, both Bob and I worked about eighteen hours a day, seven days a week. We both loved Nantucket, it's true, but we might almost as well have been running an inn in Kalamazoo or Pittsburgh, for all we got to enjoy the vacation aspects of the island.

Meanwhile, though, we *had* learned some of the ropes, and we felt sure that we could do better the following summer. We knew, for instance, that there wasn't any need to concentrate on getting reservations during the rush season, from the middle of July to the end of August, because the inn would probably be full then anyway. During those six weeks, persons seeking accommodations come knocking at your door, and are sent to you in droves by the excellent Nantucket Information Bureau, somewhat similar to a chamber of commerce. The rush season would pay all our bills and the mortgage installments. For our profit, we would have to depend on guests who came during June, the first part of July, and September. There wasn't any use to operate at all before June and after September.

Mrs. Macy told us that some inn proprietors got additional guests in June and September by giving kickbacks to taxicab drivers who picked up prospects at the steamer wharf and airport. Mrs. Macy advised against such kickbacks, which she pointed out were certainly unethical and probably illegal. In fact, whenever a cab driver in the past had suggested that Mrs. Macy pay off for favors, she had not hesitated to call the police.

Bob and I agreed that we, too, would resist kickbacks. Aside from the ethics, we were reluctant to part with any of our hard-earned receipts.

Mrs. Macy was sympathetic and amused when we complained about the general impression that we had made a fortune.

"You've got to get used to that," she chuckled in her half whisper. "All of them—even my own relatives on the island—believe I've got it buried in the back yard. I, myself, used to believe the same thing about inn-keepers, before I opened this place of mine."

"What would you think," Bob asked her, "if next summer I got my *own* cab, and met the boats in it myself during the slack times, to bring guests to Anchor Inn?"

"I'd think it was some enterprising," Mrs. Macy said. "But I don't know what the other cab drivers would think—a millionaire stealing some of their business."

"If I filled our inn, I might even steer some of my passengers to you," said Bob, "for the customary kickback, of course."

"I'll see you in jail first, you scamp," smiled Mrs. Macy.

Besides the cab, we also decided we would offer reduced rates during June and late September, and would advertise that fact in the New York and Boston newspapers.

But we could see quite plainly from our account books that no matter how well the inn did in subsequent summers, we would still need a steady source of income during the winter.

Actually, I suppose we had known this all along. Certainly neither Bob nor myself would have been content to sit back and just hibernate for eight or nine months of the year.

Fortunately, too, Bob had always had a strong urge to teach school. When he was an undergraduate at the University of North Carolina, he had thought seriously of becoming a teacher, but had finally rejected the idea because the pay scale was so low he didn't see how he could ever support a family.

We thought it would be an ideal arrangement, now, if Bob could teach school and we could run the inn during his summer vacations. First, though, he'd have to take some courses in education in order to get a teaching certificate.

Those courses would cost money. So would the taxicab and a new ironer and washing machine. I had vowed I wasn't going to go through another summer with Bob risking life and limb, not to mention destroying sheets, while wrestling with the old equipment. Also, we hoped to renovate the rooms on the third floor, and try to keep them rented.

Perhaps I'm too interested in frivolous luxuries, but I entertained hopes of getting our own personal bathtub, too. Occasionally, when there were vacancies, we had enjoyed real baths. But it was always embarrassing to emerge with that "scrubbed look," while carrying a damp towel and dirty clothes, from a bathroom that usually was rented. The guests who saw us were bound to wonder how we bathed when all our rooms were occupied. Perhaps some of them wondered whether, when they departed in the morning for the beach, we didn't sometimes slip into their tub for a quick rinse. I had better not commit myself on that matter, any further than to say there were times when I was sorely tempted.

After closing the inn in late September, Bob and I went to my family's farm at Somers, Connecticut, and earned our keep for a couple of months by helping my father get in his apple crop. I know my folks were glad to have us, and were particularly glad to have Ann, their only grandchild, whom they spoiled shamelessly. But Bob and I felt a little like charity cases, just the same. Perhaps we imagined it, but we got the impression from both of our families that the inn business was a mistake, and that we'd be better off if Bob had his old job back.

All in all, it was a busy, hectic winter. Bob went for a semester to the University of Massachusetts, at Amherst, to get the courses he needed in practice teaching and education. He did odd jobs whenever he could find them. During his Christmas vacation, he and I both went to work as extra sales clerks in a store at Springfield, Massachusetts, which is near Somers.

By spring, Bob had his teaching certificate, and we headed back to Nantucket to make the improvements on Anchor Inn. As always, we had been counting the days until we would be able to return to the island. Thanks to our various jobs, we still had almost half of the fifteen hundred dollars with which we had left Nantucket six months before.

We were both badly disappointed in the steamer trip. The passage in March bore no resemblance to summer trips, and even Bob could muster no enthusiasm for it.

In place of the large, gay, vacationing crowds, there were only about a dozen passengers, uniformly bored and glum. All of them were Nantucketers who had been on vacations to the mainland,

and I guess they were thinking about the ordeal of getting ready for the summer season, and the bigger ordeal of the summer season itself.

Almost unanimously, they flopped out full length on couches in the salon, and fell into sleep so heavy that they had to be wakened when the steamer finally reached Nantucket.

Ann, too, fell asleep, but not until she had inquired for the hundredth time why Granny and Grandpa and Auntie Janet, my sister, weren't with us. Bob and I hadn't realized that the boat's newsstand didn't operate in the winter, and so we had nothing to read. It was much too windy and bleak to go out on deck, where the salt spray was icy, so we wandered around inside, reading and digesting such framed documents as the officers' maritime licenses, the vessel's inspection certificate, instructions on how to sound the emergency alarm, man-overboard procedure, and where to find the lifejackets and how to put them on.

Every so often, a member of the crew would come through, and when he opened a door to go out on deck the wind would sweep through the overheated salon, stir up dust, and cause an immediate drop of thirty or forty degrees in temperature. Bob and I would crawl into our overcoats, but before long the salon was overheated again and we'd have to take them off. A draft under the doors left our feet cold, even though we were perspiring at forehead level.

When we went into the snack bar to get coffee, we found it manned by an uncooperative individual sitting on a chair with his heels propped up on a table.

Bob placed our order, but the counterman complained:

"Hey, this is a rest period! Ain't a guy entitled to a break in his job?"

We didn't realize it at the time, but the counterman's remarks pretty well summed up the islanders' reaction toward work. They are not afraid of work and they are not unwilling to work. But they are extremely independent about the terms of their labor; they do not approve of being bossed; they act as if they invented the rest period; and, no matter how attractive the pay, they will quit a job the moment they decide they are being imposed upon.

Disappointed that the trip to Nantucket wasn't living up to expectations, Bob was in no mood to be sassed.

"It looks to me," said Bob, "as if your whole job is a rest period and a break."

"Ain't it the truth," agreed the counterman, suddenly grinning. "You folks are Anchor, aren't you?"

"Yes, we run Anchor Inn," I put in quickly, before Bob had a chance to make any other sage observations.

"How was Florida?"

"We didn't get to Florida," I said, thinking of how we had sweated over the apple crop, and in the Springfield department store, and at various other odd jobs where we had picked up a few dollars here and there.

"We took the Caribbean cruise, instead," said Bob.

We eventually got our coffee, but not until the rest period had officially expired. Back in the salon again, we read and re-read how to put on the lifejackets. I would have tried one on, out of sheer boredom, if it hadn't been against the rules.

About thirty islanders, bundled up in drab scarves and mackinaws or greatcoats, were at the wharf to see who got off the steamer. Only one boat arrives a day in the winter, and some year-round residents make it a practice to kill time by watching her dock.

All the onlookers seemed to know who we were, but neither

Bob nor I could place more than a handful of them. They stared at us in disbelief and one old man, who obviously was expressing the sentiments of all of them, hollered:

"What are you doing here, Anchor? It ain't summer yet."

"Do tell," shivered Bob, who was more pleased than otherwise both with our new nickname of Anchor and with the stir our arrival was causing.

It surely wasn't summer. I had never felt a more dank, bone-chilling climate. You can get used to it, but it takes years.

"How was Florida?" came the question which we now considered inevitable. "Guess you people will be buying two or three inns for the coming summer, eh?"

"Your little girl has sure grown," said another one of the greeters. "Pretty as a picture, too."

We walked up toward town from the pier and ran into friendly but incredulous stares whenever we passed anyone on the street, which wasn't very often.

Three-quarters of the houses and half of the stores in the vicinity of Main Street were boarded closed, and the ratio was much higher in other parts of the town. The village, which in summertime appears charming and quaint, now looked drear and deserted, as if its adventurous inhabitants had got wind of a gold rush and departed hastily. The stay-putters seemed to be mostly old people and school-aged children. Actually, March is Nantucket's bleakest month: The scallop season, which is the winter bread and butter, is over, and it is still too early for most islanders to get to work on chores incident to the summer season. Anyone who thinks that Nantucketers are afraid of hard work, though, is welcome to try his hand at scalloping during a January gale.

We finally found a restaurant which operated in the winter. Al-

133

though I had thought I knew every store in town, I had never even noticed the cafe before. But in winter, it was the center of a good deal of activity.

Quaint restaurants are for tourists. This one, which catered to Nantucketers, featured a motif which was somebody's idea of Broadway or Hollywood. It had modernistic, chrome-trimmed furniture; a sleek, black counter; a neon-lighted juke box with colored water bubbling through glass tubes; and pale-green murals. A streamlined oil heater kept the temperature at eighty degrees, which is the target—seldom achieved, because many of the homes are old and drafty—of most Nantucketers.

Despite its efforts at sophistication, the cafe managed somehow to give off a pleasant atmosphere of small-town camaraderie. If you closed your eyes, you could almost imagine that the stream-lined heater was a pot-bellied coal stove at which loungers might squirt tobacco juice.

The waitress-proprietor gaped when we came in and quizzed us at length about Florida. After she took our order, I had an opportunity to study the murals. My favorite was the one of Brant Point Lighthouse. The artist, thoughtfully, had inserted an electric socket at the top of the lighthouse. An electric bulb, jutting out at a right angle to the mural, flashed on and off.

Anchor Inn isn't equipped for winter occupancy and there was always the danger that, if we turned on the water, the exposed pipes would burst. We moved in anyway, chose the snuggest of the guest rooms, and spent the coldest night any of us had ever experienced. We started out in twin beds and a crib, well covered with layers of blankets which smelled strongly of moth balls. Since there was no heat in the room, the sheets were icy and we simply couldn't get them warm. When Ann kept shivering, I moved her into bed with me and added her blankets to my bed.

Bob went to get more blankets, dividing them between him and me. We were still too cold to sleep, and finally Bob took all his blankets, piled them on my bed, and got in with Ann and me. As we should have known, the blankets were summer-weight, a mixture of cotton and wool. It's good business to have light blankets at a summer inn, because your guests like to write home truthfully that they are sleeping under two or three of them, and this may attract new visitors to the island.

The following morning, we ordered a large kerosene stove. I don't suppose that any other stoves had been ordered from that particular store for a couple of months, since most stove-buying takes place at the very start of winter and we were getting in at the tail-end. Thus business at the store was not exactly booming.

It seemed to pose quite a problem, nevertheless, when I suggested that the stove be delivered that same day. I had brought Ann with me, and when I showed the clerk-proprietor how purple she looked, he promised to round up a crew and get it delivered.

"I suppose," he said, "it *does* seem a little chilly after Florida. Why don't you people rent a comfortable house for a few months until it warms up?"

Fortunately, besides bringing Ann, I had remembered to leave Bob at home. This allowed me to pass over the remark smoothly and pleasantly. I smiled and professed great interest when informed that we were having a mild March, and that if I really wanted to see cold weather I should have been at Nantucket one January some years back. It seems that the harbor had frozen so solidly that people were ice-skating all the way to the end of the jetties, and the steamer couldn't get in for a week.

The price of the stove also included a standard installation charge. When three men arrived at Anchor Inn with it that afternoon, Bob did some measuring and announced that—while it would go through the front door, all right—it wouldn't go through a doorway leading from the front hall.

"I think," he told them, "you'd better take it around to the porch and bring it through the window."

All three men looked Bob over carefully.

"We're not working for you," one of them finally announced.

"I know you're not," Bob admitted amiably. "But I'm the fellow who bought the stove, and I'm just trying to save you some trouble."

"Do you aim to carry it in by yourself?"

"No," Bob assured them, "but I'm more than willing to help."

"We don't need any help."

They picked up the stove and carried it through the front door.

"I tell you," Bob insisted, "it won't get through the hall door."

They carefully lowered the stove to the floor, leaned against it, and looked Bob over carefully again.

"Who says it won't?" one of them asked.

"I do," said Bob. "I measured. You're just wasting your time."

"We ain't wasting *your* time, are we?"

"No."

"And you don't aim to install it by yourself?"

"No."

"Then would it be asking too much for you to clam up and let us install it?"

If they had known Bob as well as I do, they would have realized it was asking a great deal too much.

"You mean," said Bob, "you want me to keep my mouth shut and let you find out about it the hard way."

"We mean we want you to keep your mouth shut," roared the spokesman, "or the stove goes back to the store."

136

"All right," Bob gave in. "You don't mind if I watch though, do you?"

The three glared at him, but apparently they couldn't think of any reason why Bob shouldn't watch. He got a chair and made himself comfortable near the front door.

The men picked up the stove and carried it to the hall door. It wouldn't go through. They turned it around, and it still wouldn't go through. They laid it on its side and it still wouldn't go through. They stood it upright on the floor again, and studied the doorway. It was plain that they were exasperated.

"May I say *one* thing?" Bob asked in his most reasonable tone of voice. Apparently he thought it best not to wait for specific permission, because he continued hurriedly, "If you'll only take it out on the porch, there's a big window . . ."

"Look, friend," the spokesman interrupted icily, "your wife comes to the store and complains about your freezing to death and your daughter's freezing to death. We break our backs to rush this stove to your house, and you keep getting in our way so we can't install it for you. For the last time, do you want us to take it back to the store?"

"I don't care where you take it," hollered Bob, thoroughly exasperated now himself. "I'll tell you one thing, though. You'll never take it through that hall door."

The men shrugged and were about to carry the stove back to their truck, when I decided it was time to intercede. My sympathies in the argument were all with Bob. But, whatever happened, I wasn't going to let the stove slip out of my grasp, when it was within twenty or thirty feet of its ultimate destination.

"Let them do it their own way, Bob," I begged. "Perhaps you gentlemen would like a cup of coffee? I've got some on the stove."

The coffee break, which is not necessarily to be confused with the rest period, is another Nantucket winter-time tradition. And the men were of the opinion that after the strenuous job of carrying the one-hundred-and-fifty-pound stove from the street a few paces into Anchor Inn, a coffee break was more than overdue. They trooped into the kitchen and sat down, while I poured the coffee. Then I got Bob aside and made him solemnly swear he wouldn't say another word.

"You men install the stove any way you want to," I told them. "My husband and I realize that you know your jobs, don't we, Bob?"

Bob pressed his lips together and then said that, in view of his promise to me, he stood mute.

After the coffee, the men picked up the stove again, tried to get it through the hall door, turned it around, twisted it, angled it. Again they set it on the floor.

"More than one way to skin a cat," their spokesman assured me. They took the hall door off its hinges, but still no luck.

"More than one way to skin a cat," repeated the spokesman, but he couldn't put much conviction in it any more.

Leaving the stove where it was, they departed in their truck and returned an hour later with a box of tools. Painstakingly, they took off the outer case of the stove, and then lifted up its innards. I could see, and I'm sure they could, too, that the innards weren't going to get through, either. Taking Bob with me before he forgot his promise, I went into the kitchen to fix another pot of coffee.

After the five of us had had our second cups of coffee, they put the stove back together again.

"You should have known better," the spokesman told me accusingly, "than to buy a stove that was too big to get through that door."

138

"Gee, I'm sorry," I said, willing to plead guilty to anything as long as I didn't lose the stove. "I suppose it was stupid of me, but it simply never occurred to me."

"You know what we're going to have to do now?" he asked. "We're going to have to take this thing in through the porch window."

Nudging Bob to keep quiet, I exclaimed, "Now, *there's* a good idea."

The spokesman reached over suddenly and rumpled Bob's hair, and the action somehow took all of the tension out of the room. "Go ahead, Anchor," he urged Bob, "say it."

"More than one way," grinned Bob, "to skin a cat."

10 ~ Antiquing at the Dump

Even a Nantucket with a ghost-town atmosphere and a marrow-freezing climate had charms that caused us to fall in love with the place all over again. The island claims a winter-time population of thirty-five hundred, but there are probably less than three thousand persons there in March because many Nantucketers take their vacations in that month.

Between our chores, we found time to drive on the moors, to visit Siasconset and Madaket, to bundle up warm in recently acquired mackinaws and walk the empty beaches on clear, blue days. At night, we sometimes went to a movie at the Dreamland, and then dropped by Coffin's Drug Store for a soda—ice-cream and tonic, as it's known on Nantucket—with the night owls.

We redecorated and rearranged the third floor so as to make three bedrooms and a bath. The equipment for the bathroom was already there and connected, so all we had to do was to put up some interior walls and doors. Still, it was our first experience with major carpentry, and we were quite well satisfied with the results, which would provide additional revenue.

When this job was completed, we got an electric sander and started on the downstairs floors. The transformation was really remarkable. As layer after layer of chipped paint was ground into dust, the wide, red-orange planks emerged with a coppery glow that can't be counterfeited and that only time can produce.

An eighty-three-year-old neighbor had told me that when she was a girl, Anchor Inn was an abandoned house, with broken windows and with doors that slammed open and shut in the wind. She said the children of the neighborhood had been afraid to walk past our house at night, because derelict seamen sometimes camped there. As we sanded down the floor around the hearths, we found deep axe marks in some of the planks. Bob guessed that the seamen may have dragged wood into the house, and chopped it into kindling in front of the fireplaces.

The axe marks didn't detract from the atmosphere of the inn. Certainly the overall effect of the sanded floors was to add tremendously to the inn's antique appearance. And, believe me, if bathrooms are bread and butter at a New England resort inn, an antique appearance is cake and frosting.

The paint and wood dust covered every inch of us, every inch of the inn, all of our furniture and most of our food. It even got in the refrigerator. We ate it, wore it, breathed it, and slept in it. After the sanding was finished, it took me two weeks of washing and vacuuming to get rid of most of the dust. And four weeks later, Bob still alleged that he was combing the dust out of his hair, brushing it out of his teeth, shaking it out of his clothes and blowing it out of his nostrils.

Meanwhile, I had been standing firm on my insistence that a

bathtub be installed for our own use. Since our savings were rapidly disappearing, Bob now thought it might be a smart idea to wait for another year.

"It'll cost five hundred dollars if it will cost a cent," Bob declared. "People are always underestimating the cost of installing a bath—all the books on renovating old houses say that! And we simply can't afford it."

"Suppose," I said, "we could get it done for a hundred dollars?"

"If we could get a bathtub installed for a hundred dollars," Bob scoffed, "I'd say let's get one for us and let's get one for every guest room."

The reason I had mentioned the figure of a hundred dollars was that I had secretly brought in a plumber to look over the kitchen, and he had told me he really might be able to install a tub for that amount.

My plan was to put the tub in the space then occupied by the kitchen dish closet. This would involve moving one of the closet's walls a distance of three feet, which wasn't a very big job, and also moving a gas cookstove near the wall. The plumber had dug in the yard and had found that a soil pipe actually passed right under the dish closet. He also told me that he had a small second-hand bathtub, which would fit into the enlarged closet. After some bargaining, the plumber agreed to sell me the tub for ten dollars.

I interpreted Bob's remarks about hundred-dollar installations as tantamount to endorsement of my plans. I thought it best, however, not to disclose those plans until I could actually confront Bob with something of a *fait accompli,* in the nature of a tool-bearing plumber ready to go to work.

I drove over to see the plumber, Mr. Goshen, and he promised to "come tomorrow for sure." Then I spent most of the next day trying to keep Bob in a good humor, so that he wouldn't rebel when the plumber showed up—but Mr. Goshen didn't appear. Like most Nantucketers, Mr. Goshen was such a pleasant chap he apparently didn't have the heart to inform me that he was working on another job and wouldn't be able to get to us for weeks. I telephoned him—when Bob wasn't around—and stretched the truth a little by saying that my husband was most eager to have the work get started. Mr. Goshen kept assuring me that he'd see me tomorrow, and I kept trying to soften up Bob with waffles for breakfast and pies for dessert.

By the time Mr. Goshen finally arrived, I had long since given him up, and stopped trying to keep Bob in a perpetual, overfed good humor. In fact, after weeks of slaving on the meals, I had let the pendulum swing the other way and was doing a minimum job of cookery. Bob, spoiled by special dishes I had spread before him, had been especially annoyed that morning to find that his breakfast consisted of cold cereal, instant coffee and some toast he was expected to fix for himself. Bob answered Mr. Goshen's knock, a few minutes after breakfast, and by the time I arrived on the scene the conversation was already fairly spirited.

"I tell you," Bob was saying, "there's some mistake. There's nothing wrong with our pipes, and we don't want anybody messing with them. When we need a plumber, we send for one. And when we don't need a plumber, we don't expect to have one of them shoving his foot into the front door as if he were selling brushes or working his way through college."

"All I know," replied Mr. Goshen, "is that your wife told me, every day for two weeks, that you were having fits because you couldn't take a bath."

"And I tell you," hollered Bob, "it must have been somebody

144

else's wife. I never went for two weeks in my life without a bath."

"Come right in, Mr. Goshen," I urged, pushing Bob aside. "I see you've already met my husband."

"I've had the pleasure," remarked Mr. Goshen.

"I want you to tell my husband that you can give us a bathtub, all installed, for only a hundred dollars."

"Let him put in his own bathtub," said Mr. Goshen. "I've got more work than I can do, anyway."

"I'm sorry if I was impolite," Bob put in hastily. "I didn't know my wife had asked you to come."

"Go ahead and tell him, Mr. Goshen," I suggested. "He's apologized."

"That's okay," Mr. Goshen smiled good-naturedly. "But I never said the job could be done for a hundred dollars. I said it could be done for a hundred dollars if everything went well."

"Do you think everything will go well?" Bob asked.

"You can't be sure of anything about the plumbing in these old houses until you tap into it. The cost might be much more than that."

"In other words," said Bob, glaring at me, "no one could *guarantee* to do the job for a hundred dollars. You can't guarantee it yourself, for instance."

"Sure can't," the plumber agreed.

"Let's just skip it then, if you don't mind," said Bob. "I'm sorry you had to make the trip over here. I think I owe you a debt of gratitude, too, for some of the best breakfasts I've had since I was married."

"No trouble," said Mr. Goshen. "I'll tell you the truth, I dread going into the plumbing of these old houses."

"Listen, Bob," I begged, "I've got the whole business figured to the last penny. The tub itself is only going to cost ten dollars. It will go in the dish closet, and we can help Mr. Goshen move the closet wall."

"No," said Bob.

"Ann's too big to fit in a dishpan this year," I insisted, "and I'm not going to take another spongebath as long as I live. I tell you what, *I'll* guarantee the job can be done for a hundred dollars."

"Do you think there's a pretty fair chance it could be done for that amount," Bob asked Mr. Goshen again.

"There's a chance, but you're the ones who will have to take the risk if it runs more than that."

"I'll guarantee it," I promised. "Look, Bob, I really mean this: *I want that bathtub.*"

"If it costs more than a hundred dollars," Bob surrendered, "you're going to pay for it out of your allowance. Come on in then, Mr. Goshen, and I'll give you a hand."

Since I had won the argument, I refrained from asking the obvious question, which was "What allowance?"

Let me say that Mr. Goshen is a good, honest plumber. We've called him on numerous occasions since the installation of my ten-dollar bathtub. He's skilled in his work and will come at a moment's notice when there's a real emergency like a broken pipe. He was as distressed as we at the chain reaction which was set off when he started tapping into our old gas and water mains.

When Mr. Goshen unhooked the stove, the gas pipe simply disintegrated.

"How much will that cost?" Bob asked.

"Ten dollars or so, if we're lucky," said Mr. Goshen. "If not, a whole lot more."

We weren't lucky. After Bob pulled up the kitchen linoleum,

146

and two floorboards to get at the gas pipe, we could see that the gas main itself was rusting to pieces. Mr. Goshen gave the main one gentle poke with a work-gloved finger, and the pipe crumbled before our eyes.

"How much?" asked Bob.

"It was a good thing we discovered that!" said Mr. Goshen.

"How much?" repeated Bob.

"We'll have to replace it all the way to the meter," sighed the plumber. "It's something that had to be done whether or not you had a new bathtub."

"I admit that," said Bob. "How much?"

"We'll have to take up most of the floor," Mr. Goshen said. "Since you don't have a basement, there's no other way to get at it. Four hundred dollars—maybe more."

"There goes my next week's allowance," I groaned.

"It wasn't your fault." Bob sheered me up. "It had to be fixed."

I wasn't so sure. I've come to the conclusion that what you don't know about rusted plumbing won't hurt you.

We got a carpenter to help tear up the floor, and then to help put the floor back down again. By the time we had bought new linoleum, moved the stove exactly three feet, and hooked the stove to a new gas pipe which in turn was hooked to a new gas main, the bill was six hundred dollars. And we hadn't even started on the bathroom.

By then, I had become reconciled to putting up with another summer of spongebaths. But Bob decided that, since we'd already spent six hundred dollars, we might as well get something out of our investment.

We moved the closet wall without incident. But when the pipes from the tub were connected to the hot and cold water pipes,

there were additional disintegrations, additional floor disman-
tlings, and some entirely new hole-pokings in the wall. And,
finally, thirty-five feet of sewer pipe had to be replaced. We arranged to pay off the charges in installments. If the cost had been
one hundred and fifty dollars or two hundred dollars, Bob probably would never have let me hear the end of it. As it was, he
mentioned it only once, and then dropped the subject.

He was eating breakfast and adding up the bills, the morning
after the job was completed, when he mentioned the cost of the
bath for the last time. "More waffles, honey?" I had inquired.
"There's oodles of batter."

"You know, honey," said Bob, "I've added everything up, and
we are probably the only people in the world who ever spent one
thousand and ninety dollars to install a miniature, ten-dollar bathtub."

But when he said it, he smiled—or at any rate, he tried to. I
put another waffle on his plate, and poured some more batter into
the iron.

Mrs. Macy, who spent the winters managing a tourist court near
Jacksonville, returned to Nantucket. It was good to have her back
again, and to watch the other inns on Centre Street begin to
come to life as preparations were made for the opening of the
season.

Although Bob and I were living pretty much on credit, we
managed to turn in our small washing machine as a down-payment
on a commercial-sized washer and an automatic ironer. Bob had
hoped that the man at the appliance store would also allow us
something on our old ironer, and I, too, entertained such a hope
when I saw how carefully the appliance man examined that antique.

148

"It *is* an ironer, isn't it?" the appliance man asked. "Have you been operating *that?*"

"Sure," said Bob. "It works like a charm. I haven't used it yet this year, but I'll show you. Do you happen to have a match on you? Perhaps you'd better stand back while I throw this switch."

I edged silently toward the door, but the appliance man beat me to it.

"Don't you touch that thing while I'm around," he shouted from the middle of the tulip bed.

Since we couldn't get a trade-in allowance on the old ironer, Mrs. Macy suggested that we offer it for sale in the want ad columns of *The Inquirer and Mirror* and *The Nantucket Town Crier*. She explained that no Nantucketer ever threw anything away until he had tried first to sell it and then to trade it.

We knew that she spoke from first-hand experience in this regard, since she had recently purchased for thirty-five dollars a ninth or tenth-hand, pot-type oil stove advertised in the newspapers. Within a week, two explosions caused by back-drafts had twice blackened her living room with soot and twice set fire to her drapes. After removing the drapes and all evidence of the soot, she polished the stove carefully and then inserted an ad which read:

"For Sale: Dependable, slightly used oil stove. Good as new. Keeps whole house warm as toast. Sacrifice."

She asked sixty-five dollars for the stove, and finally sold it for forty-five.

"I really lost money, when you consider the cost of the drapes," she explained ruefully.

Although Bob had been willing enough to try to palm off the ironer on the appliance man, he didn't have the heart to try to palm it off on anyone else.

"The appliance man would have had sense enough to junk it, after he had looked it over," Bob explained. "I don't believe I could sleep nights if I knew I was responsible for anyone actually trying to operate the thing. Besides, there's no way a candid ad could be written, without getting those issues of the paper banned from the mails for obscenities."

So Bob borrowed a truck to cart the ironer out to the town dump, on the moors near the Madaket Road.

A number of Nantucketers, including us, case the dump fairly regularly to see if there's anything worth salvaging. Since there's no free collection of trash by the town, many persons also pile their rubbish into cars and deliver it personally.

Thus the dump is somewhat of a community center, although an extraordinarily odoriferous one, where friends and acquaintances meet on the most democratic of terms. The activity of salvaging is sometimes dignified with the term of "antiquing." Young children like the place, because it abounds with friendly seagulls, grown fat on garbage. And men sometimes meet there at night to shoot rats with .22 rifles. This rat-shooting is a favorite winter sport, requiring no hunting license and subject to no season restrictions. The men sit quietly in their cars with the lights out, and sometimes perhaps a bottle changes hands. Then, suddenly, all the headlights flash on at the same time, and the sportsmen blast away.

The best "antiquing" time occurs in late June and early September, when the summer people are opening or closing their houses and getting rid of things they no longer want. Bob and I once found a beautiful mirror with plate glass nearly half an inch thick; and once lost a shovel which Bob had brought along to clear some rubbish from the back of our car. A neighbor of ours found three pieces of old pewter, which he cleaned up and sold at a handsome price.

A paid dump-keeper, who is on duty during the week, has first rights on everything left there. But he isn't on duty Sundays or after about five o'clock in the afternoons, so most "antiquing" occurs in his absence. The drivers of rubbish trucks, who pick up trash for a fee and are employed mostly by the summer people, have even better pickings than the dump-keeper. One of these drivers carefully cleans, at the source, any article he thinks might be useful. Such articles ride up in the front seat with him, until he returns home, when he centers them on his neat lawn. There's no sign saying they're for sale or suggesting a price, but Nantucketers know that he's waiting for an offer. The turnover is rapid, and an article rarely stays on display for more than twelve hours.

As Bob drove up toward the dump in the borrowed truck, bearing the dangerous old ironer, one of the "antiquers" waved him down.

"Hold up, son," said the man, an old-timer with a tobacco-stained mustache, oil-skin jacket, and rubber boots. "What's that you've got there, an ironer?"

"Sure is," Bob replied.

"You aim to throw it away?"

"Calc'late I would," said Bob, who sometimes takes seriously this native son business.

"If you steer it over to my place in that truck, I'll give you three lobsters (pronounced laubstas) for it. You kin follie me. That's my car down the road."

"I wouldn't want to cheat you," said Bob. "This thing's no good."

151

"What do you mean, no good?" the old-timer protested. "It's just what I've been lookin' high and low fer, boy!"

"Not if you're looking for an ironer," Bob said. "This thing might blow up on you."

"What would I be wantin' with an ironer, son? I'm lookin' fer an anchor fer a lobster pot."

II—High Altitude Puttying

For the two weeks before we were to open for our second season, Bob and I worked steadily painting all the shutters. Bob removed them by leaning out of the windows and lifting them from their hinges. Since neither of us like high places, I suggested—and he quickly agreed—that it would be good insurance on the second and third floor for me to stand directly behind him, and hang onto his belt.

Once the shutters were brought in through the windows, we carried them into the back yard and applied the paint. The job went smoothly, except on one occasion when Ann sat in and upset a gallon of green paint. (A year later, after the incident had slipped my mind, I was digging in the yard to plant a rose bush and discovered what I thought was a rare, green mineral deposit. I called Bob excitedly, pointed it out, and didn't neglect to cite the experience I had gained while employed in chemical re-

search. Naturally, I was deflated when Bob reminded me I was
digging where Ann had the accident.)

The shutters were hand-made to fit the old windows which
varied fractionally in size. Since the shutters were numbered, we
hadn't anticipated any trouble in putting them back. However,
for some reason, the numbers didn't correspond with those on
the windows. Bob sometimes had to try thirty shutters before he
found the one that fit. Needless to say, we re-numbered them before we took them down again.

One other job we had intended to do ourselves was renewing
the putty in the windows. It was so dried out and cracked that
many of the panes were leaking. Since our first guests were about
to arrive, we decided we'd better get professional help with the
puttying. Also, there was again the element of height. The windows couldn't very well be repaired from inside the house. I
was willing to putty only the first floor windows. Bob was willing
to get on our rickety ladder and do the second-story windows,
but not the third. He concurred enthusiastically with my proposal
that we hire glaziers or steeplejacks to ascend into the strato-
sphere.

We discovered, as we had in the case of the plumber, that Nantucket glaziers are so pleasant and obliging they wouldn't dream
of disappointing you by saying right to your face that your requests don't always fit in with their own plans and intentions.

Fred and Jonah, buddies, partners, eligible bachelors, and master
glaziers, indicated they'd show up at the stroke of eight the following morning to work for us—or "help you out," as the islanders
prefer to say. We didn't really expect them, and of course they
didn't come.

We had learned by then that pressure from a prospective em-
ployer never speeds the arrival of a prospective helpmate, and may

indeed delay it. Also, it would have aroused hard feelings if he had sought other glaziers, after Fred and Jonah had agreed to do the job. We bided our time, went ahead with the low-level puttying, and awaited their convenience.

When they finally appeared, five or six days later, the first of our guests had arrived. This was just as well, since we intended to pay the glaziers by the hour, and we needed the rent receipts to meet the payroll. We put our few initial guests in the rooms whose windows we had already puttied, so that they wouldn't be bothered by workmen.

Fred was a big, handsome man, with a local reputation for being a hell-rake. I liked him, after I got to know him, but I thought he rather overdid his efforts to live up to his reputation. Jonah, raw-boned and not the ladies' man type, worshiped him. Jonah would have liked nothing better than to be a hell-rake himself, and was always in there pitching, but his appearance was against him. I was crazy about Jonah, right from the start.

Because of the condition of our finances, we hoped to get the maximum amount of "help" per hour from our glaziers. Bob decided that he'd work along with them—but at a lower story— to discourage soldiering on the job. I decided to keep coffee perpetually hot on the stove, to discourage trips to town for the coffee-break.

Fred and Jonah welcomed Bob as a member of the glazing team. They were both sick and tired of glazing, day in and day out, anyway. They weren't half so interested in the money involved as getting our job done with the least possible effort.

They spent the first hour examining and criticizing the windows we had tackled before their arrival. Their joint opinion, expressed repeatedly but with good-natured tolerance, was that we had "played holy hell." We hadn't painted the wood before we had put on the putty, we had applied too much putty, and we hadn't packed the putty down firmly enough.

"Do you mean that what my wife and I have done has to be pulled out and done all over again by you fellows?" Bob asked.

"Gawd, no," Fred hastened to assure us, appalled by the prospect of this additional work. "It ain't perfect to work astern of, but your work ain't *that* bad. In fact, the closer I look at it, the more I think it's really pretty shipshape, don't you Jonah?"

"I'd say," said Jonah, also completely changing his tune, "that you and Mrs. Anchor did a some shipshape job, Bawb."

The next hour was spent in scolding us for not taking proper care of our paint, paint brushes, and putty. Meanwhile, there were three interruptions by off-islanders, for whom the two glaziers had promised to work that morning. In each case, Fred and Jonah said they'd show up the following morning, for sure.

Bob offered to go uptown to get some new materials, but Fred and Jonah shook their heads. It goes against the grain of Nantucketers to see waste of any kind, and the glaziers wouldn't hear of our throwing away cans of partially hardened paint and putty. They strained the paint through cheesecloth and added turpentine. They painstakingly stirred linseed oil into the putty. There wasn't any use for us to hint that it might be cheaper to get new materials, rather than pay for the time spent in reclaiming the old. The point was—and I'm sure their Quaker ancestors would have approved—that we were "making do with what we had."

When Fred, Jonah, and Anchor—also sometimes known as Bawb—finally went to work, their progress was slow. Of the three, Fred was the talker and, from what I overheard of the conversation, was also a fascinating combination of Romeo and Walter Winchell. His stories certainly weren't meant for my ears, but he had to tell them in a loud voice, so that they would carry down the ladder to Bob. The trouble was that Fred's stories were so interesting that not only Jonah, but also Bob, who was paying the bill, sometimes stopped puttying for as long as ten minutes at a stretch, so as not to miss a word.

Fred, who had served a hitch in the Marines, outlined in some detail a number of his love affairs on Nantucket, on the mainland and in foreign countries. He gave his considered and often allegedly experienced opinion about the morals of most of the island females, young and not so young. Of the male population, he professed to know who was misbehaving and with whom, and how each had made his money, if any, and how much. It appeared that most of the wealthy male islanders had been so short of cash at one time or another that they couldn't afford even the most economical kind of home cooking. At any rate, Fred's favorite expression was that he had known each of them when "he didn't have a pot to cook his beans in."

Jonah must have heard the stories before, but he stood with poised putty-knife while he vicariously enjoyed them all over again. Fred, of course, had to stop glazing to provide the proper gestures, some of which might have interested Dr. Kinsey. And Bob was so frankly entranced, since he knew many of the principals of the stories, that it never occurred to him to tell Fred to quit gabbing and get back to work.

As for me, down in the kitchen and occasionally looking out the back door to observe progress, I may as well admit that I wasn't getting much housework done, either.

All in all, the three glaziers didn't accomplish a great deal that first day. In fact, the system of having Bob serve as a working member of the team probably slowed things much more than it helped. Beside Fred's stories, which Bob's very presence encouraged, there was the matter of someone setting the pace. Fred and Jonah reasoned that, even though they were being paid and Bob wasn't, it was unfair to expect them to work any harder than he. Every time Bob had to quit puttying to perform some other job, Fred and Jonah quit too, and took a rest period until he was ready to resume.

After two days of this gigantic boondoggle, Jonah showed up the next morning without Fred, who had some work he wanted to do on his motorboat. When I protested that the job would now drag on for most of the summer, Jonah assured me that he and his other partner, Bawb, would have the task done in no time.

Actually, Jonah was miserable without Fred, and he buckled down to finish up in a hurry, so that he could rejoin his buddy. In the absence of his regular partner, Jonah apparently thought it his duty to substitute as raconteur, but at least he puttied while he talked. His stories, based largely on wishful thinking, didn't need illustration with gestures, anyway. As for local gossip, Jonah's was confined to improbable bedroom scenes he said he'd witnessed in the past, while puttying.

There was certainly nothing in Jonah's stories to make Bob pause in his work, either.

Both Fred and Jonah were fearless when it came to ladders, ascending one-handed to dizzy heights and then, without holding on at all, leaning far out to paint and putty. So now, when it finally was time to tackle the highest windows, Jonah put the ladder on our angled porch roof, chocked it haphazardly, and asked Bob to hold it with his feet. Then Jonah grabbed paint and putty cans and nonchalantly went up, while the ladder sagged and swayed. When he got to the top, the ladder wasn't quite where he wanted it, so he heaved at it and slid it over. I couldn't bear to watch him, and even Bob, at the base of the ladder, didn't look up very often.

Jonah stayed up there, working steadily, for an hour. Then he came down, stepped onto the porch roof, moved the ladder, and stretched.

"I'm tired," he said.

"I'll bet you are," Bob sympathized. "I know it's no fun at the top of the ladder."

Jonah handed Bob the cans and placed his feet at the bottom of the ladder.

"Your turn, Bawb," he said.

"What do you mean?" Bob inquired.

"Up you go. I'm tired."

"Me?" Bob shouted. "Way up there?"

"What's the idea?" asked Jonah. "You don't expect me to do *all* the work, do you, while you stand down there taking things easy?"

"We'll take a rest period for as long as you want," said Bob, "and then you go back up, okay?"

"No," said Jonah. "You're not going to give me all the dirty work, while you loaf."

"But you're *paid* to 'help out,'" Bob explained, "and I'm not."

"You're some card, Bawb," laughed Jonah. "Are you trying to tell me I ought to pay you to fix your own windows?"

"I don't mean that at all," Bob protested. "The thing is that I don't like high ladders."

"You'll never make a good window man, Bawb, until you get used to high ladders."

"Even if I never have a pot to cook my beans in," Bob said positively, "I'm not going up that ladder. That's final."

"Bawb," Jonah said not unkindly, "Fred and I learned you a lot about puttying, but I can't learn you to go up ladders unless you go up them. Now start climbing, or I quit. That's final, too."

He braced his feet on the bottom of the ladder. "Up you go."

"You mean climb?" Bob chattered.

"Climb!"

"How about some coffee first, eh?"

"Climb!"

Bob climbed, holding the cans with one hand and wrapping his other arm all the way around each rung as he ascended. The ladder swayed and its top shifted. Bob froze for a few moments, but he went up. When he got within stretching distance of the window, he stopped, got a scissor-grip on the ladder with his legs, and reached up to chip away the old putty. But Jonah wouldn't let him get away with that.

"Go all the way up, Bawb," he called, "until the window's even with your chest."

"I think it's more comfortable working up over my head," quavered Bob.

"Up," ordered Jonah, "or I'll walk away from the bottom of the ladder."

Bob didn't hesitate to go up.

"That's it," Jonah commended him. "I'll make a good window man of you if it kills me."

It was apparent that Bob didn't like it up there at all, and that if he was worrying about anybody's forthcoming demise it wasn't Jonah's. No boa constrictor could have wrapped itself much more thoroughly around an object than Bob wrapped himself around the various rungs of the ladder. But he started to paint and then putty. Jonah, drawing a master glazier's pay for holding the ladder, called me to ask if it would be too much trouble to bring him a cup of coffee.

Since it was still early in the season, none of our third-floor rooms were rented. But after puttying for a few minutes, Bob made believe he had discovered something intensely interesting behind a third-floor window. He'd lean over a little—not far, because he was too tightly wrapped around the ladder—and press his nose against the window pane. Then he'd draw back hurriedly as if he was afraid of being seen.

Jonah immediately evinced great interest.

"You didn't tell me that room was rented," Jonah stage-whispered up the ladder through cupped hands.

Bob was afraid to look down, so he couldn't stage-whisper back. And it would have spoiled the act for him to have shouted. Instead, he waved the putty-knife impatiently, to indicate that Jonah had better be quiet, and quickly pressed his nose to the window again. Then he drew back and puttied some more.

"I'm rested now," Jonah stage-whispered. "Come on down, Bawb, and I'll take over."

Bob puttied and peeked a few more minutes, while Jonah became increasingly restless.

"All right, Bawb. You proved you ain't afraid of high ladders. Come on down."

Bob puttied a few more strokes.

"I'm going to start jiggling the ladder if you don't come down, Bawb," Jonah warned. "You're paying me to putty, not to hold the ladder. I ain't no apprentice boy, just learning the trade."

Bob stopped treating the ladder as if it were Laocoön, and climbed shakily down.

"How about another cup of coffee?" he asked Jonah.

"No, thanks," said Jonah, who was eager to get up the ladder. "Let's get this job finished."

"I've got to go inside for a minute. I'll be right back."

"Well, make it snappy, Bawb. Remember, it's your money."

Bob went into the house, and reappeared a few minutes later. He climbed onto the porch roof and held the ladder, while Jonah ascended hastily to the top.

I thought I knew what Bob had been up to, and after a while I disappeared into the house and climbed the stairs to the third floor. Stealthily cracking open a bedroom door, I looked in.

The bathroom door, which opened from the opposite side of the bedroom, was partially ajar. I could see that Bob had turned on the bathroom light and I could hear that he had left a faucet running. Cold water, I hoped. Draped fetchingly on the bedroom side of the bathroom doorknob was a pair of my briefest panties. My laciest slip and a brassiere so large it looked as if it might have been borrowed from Mrs. Macy's clothesline were laid out on the bed.

Jonah puttied a total of nine hours that day, and when he was through the job was finished. After shifting the ladder for the sixth time to the window that offered the best view, he finally gave up in disgust and limped down, utterly exhausted.

"Either you played a dirty trick on me, Bawb," he sighed, "or some beautiful creature is drownded."

12 ~ See Nantucket with a Gal

Improving the inn and installing my bathtub had cost so much that Bob decided it would be out of the question to buy a taxicab.

I suppose I should have learned my lesson from the bathtub episode. Just the same, I did some private investigating and discovered that a taxi license costs only fifty cents. Bargains are extremely rare on the island, and this was one bargain I couldn't resist.

As Bob patiently pointed out, when I hurried home to exhibit my purchase, we were in the taxi business except for one detail—we didn't have a taxi.

It would be a mistake to assume that I had overlooked this detail. Knowing Bob as I do, I felt sure he'd manage to get a taxi somehow, once he was confronted with the actuality of a license.

He didn't disappoint me, either.

"Here we go again," he sighed after studying the license. "I have a feeling that it may not be especially shrewd to plunge some two thousand dollars further into debt to protect a fifty-cent investment. But let's go talk to the automobile dealers."

The upshot was that, within a couple of hours, we had turned in our limping, five-year-old sedan for a new Ford Ranch Wagon, which had been delivered to the dealer only two days before.

Our new car was, in fact, the first all-metal station wagon of its make to arrive on the island. Although it came from a manufacturer in the "low-price field"—if you can call twenty-four hundred dollars a low price—it was sleek, roomy and handsome. It also was loaded with just about every accessory except a raccoon tail and a Confederate flag.

We intended to use it both as our own personal automobile and as a taxi. Since the tourist season was just getting underway, we were counting on the station wagon to pay for itself by helping immediately to fill the inn, as well as by the fares Bob would collect.

As Bob drove our new purchase from the dealer's garage to Anchor Inn, we attracted somewhat less attention among Nantucketers—but not much less—than if we had ridden along the streets in tandem, and Lady Godiva fashion, on a zebra. Looking out the back window, I could see groups of islanders forming on the sidewalks, pointing and nodding confirmation to their suspicions of our affluence.

And when I walked the couple of blocks to Main Street an hour or so later to do some shopping, I discovered that word of our purchase had preceded me to the grocery store where we trade.

"I'll say one thing for you and Bawb," the girl at the cash register said for me and Bawb, "you may not live high, but you do spend it —or *some* of it, anyway—right here on the island. Are you buying liver again, Barbara? You and Bawb must *like* liver, that's some sure. Should I charge it?"

"Please," I said. I was tempted to tell her that I couldn't have paid cash for the liver even if I wanted to, because the purchase of a taxi license earlier that morning had taken my last fifty cents. However, the intelligence that we were in the taxi business still had not been relayed along Main Street, and I thought it wise not to initiate the report.

By the time I got home again, Bob had almost finished lettering a cardboard "TAXI" sign for the windshield. He explained that he didn't want anything to be painted on the station wagon itself.

"This way," Bob added, "we can put up the sign on the windshield when we're looking for passengers. When we're using the car for pleasure, we can take down the sign and we won't be bothered by a lot of people hollering 'taxi' at us and trying to crawl into the back seat."

It made sense to me. So Ann and I went out and watched him fasten the sign to the windshield.

"I guess I'd better run down and meet the boat," Bob told us. "I'm going to try to pick out passengers who look as if they don't have room reservations any place and bring them here. I'll have this place filled up in no time."

"Can I go too?" asked Ann, which was a question she posed no more than twenty or thirty times on an average day.

"No, you can't," said Bob. "Daddy's going to be so crowded with passengers that there won't be any room."

He disappeared in the direction of the Ocean House, where President Ulysses S. Grant once slept, if he wasn't kept awake by the foghorns. I hoped that Bob might pick up a fare in front of the Ocean House, but no one waved him down.

Our telephone started ringing almost as soon as I got back into the house.

"Is this Mrs. Anchor?" asked an indignant and strange female voice.

I admitted that it was.

"Didn't I just see your husband drive by my house with a new car and a taxi sign on it?"

"You may have," I said. "Who's this?"

"Never mind, except that my husband makes a *living* by driving a taxicab. Do you and your husband want to get *all* the money that tourists bring here?"

I was trying to frame a non-profane but suitably impolite answer when she hung up the phone.

As I found out later, Bob had threaded his way through the traffic to the very end of the wharf—past the Yacht Club, where tea and cocktails were being served under gay umbrellas on the lawn; past Lucky Pierre's, a new chi-chi restaurant and hamburger house; past the shoppes that rent British bicycles to Bronx excursionists wearing Bermuda shorts, Basque berets, and Hollywood sun glasses; and past the Skipper, an unfrocked schooner, mastless, chained with permanent hawsers, and serving as a quaint tearoom. The schooner, having been forced by the times to trade perilous adventure for fettered security, seems to me to symbolize the changes which a hundred years have brought to the brave whaling capital of the world.

Pulling into the restricted area reserved for cabs, Bob had backed professionally into a taxi space closest to the steamer's gangplank to await her arrival. A good many cabs were parked nearby, with the drivers huddled happily around a car radio. The Boston Red Sox—beau ideal of all red-blooded Nantucketers who sometimes would pool their savings and charter a plane to take them to a game—were giving the despised Yankees their well-deserved lumps.

Since Bob had backed in, the assembled drivers hadn't noticed the sign on our windshield. They greeted him with good-natured reproof.

"You can't park *there*, Anchor," one of them told him, "even if you have got a new buggy. That space is reserved for taxis. Some of your folks coming on the steamer?"

Bob grinned and shook his head.

"I heard you bought that all-metal job that was shipped to Gordon's a couple of days ago," said another. "I was looking at it in his garage. She's a beauty all right. Paid cash for her, didn't you Bawb?"

"Gold," Bob nodded solemnly.

"You've still got to move her before the steamer docks," insisted the first. "Who are you meeting, Anchor?"

"Nobody in particular," said Bob. "The same people you fellows are meeting. And I don't have to move the car, either. Come here and take a look."

He pointed proudly at the windshield and the group moved forward to read the sign.

"You may now extend the warm hand of welcome to a new brother in the hard-working fraternity of cab drivers," Bob joked. "You boys will probably have to give me some pointers, because I'm green at the game."

The group studied the sign in silence, and exchanged glances. But Bob still didn't get the idea that they weren't rejoicing over his competition.

"Barb and I hope we can fill the inn and pick up some money on the side," he said. "How's this? 'Taxi! Mister! Taxi! Most folks hanker to stay at the Anchor.'"

Nobody laughed or said anything and Bob couldn't figure out why the act was falling so completely flat. He decided to try again.

"How's this, then: 'Here it is folks, the only all-steel Ranch Wagon taxi on Nantucket.' Is that any better?"

It wasn't any better. If anything, it was worse. Bob usually gets along well with everybody, so it took him a few moments to realize that the members of the taxi fraternity were not only neglecting to extend him the warm hand of fellowship, but had blackballed him to the last man.

The drivers drifted silently back to the car radio, and Bob joined them there. Because one conversational gambit had never failed in the past, Bob used it now.

"How are the Sox doing?" he asked.

"Winnin'," someone finally volunteered grudgingly.

"What's the matter with you guys?" Bob demanded. "Did you think I was making fun of cab drivers or something when I pretended I was practicing calling out 'taxi'?"

"No, it ain't that, Bawb," one of the drivers told him. "But we've got a hard enough time getting fares as it is. And you already *got* a summer business."

"I've also got a new taxi," Bob explained stubbornly, "and I've got to pay for it. And I'm *going* to pay for it."

"Not in that space you're parked, you ain't going to pay for it," the same driver said.

"Who," Bob inquired angrily, "says I'm not?"

It developed that they all said he was not. The choice parking spaces near the end of the dock had long since been rented and assigned to various cab operators. Free parking space for taxis, on a first-come-first-served basis, was provided far down the dock, away from the gangplank.

See Nantucket with a Gal

I don't think the cab drivers had really enjoyed deflating Bob. Perhaps, if anything, they had let him down fairly gently. But he felt ridiculous, just the same, when he drove away from the choicest taxi location and took his place way down the line in the free area. This time he parked the station wagon nose in, so that our taxi sign would be seen. The cab drivers flanking him in the other free spaces didn't welcome him any more cordially than had the first group. But this time, at any rate, he didn't rush out expecting the warm hand of fellowship.

When the steamer finally arrived, it became immediately apparent that most of the passengers were being met by friends who had their own automobiles. We ourselves had always made it a point to meet members of our families or close friends who were arriving from the mainland. That had seemed to be a pleasant tradition. Now Bob recognized it as an abomination, designed to cheat cab drivers out of deserved sources of revenue.

Those passengers who weren't being personally met were grabbed off quickly by the taxis in the rented spaces. Some of these taxis were seven-passenger limousines, and their drivers didn't depart until every seat was filled, with various fares going to different destinations and luggage overflowing from racks on the top.

The only steamer passengers who walked as far as the free-taxi-parking area were those who intended to walk all the way to their destination, and who had already fought off a score or so of eager drivers further up the line.

None of the ten or twelve cabs in the free space along with Bob got a single passenger, although if anything they solicited business even more conscientiously than the drivers near the gangplank.

Knowing that the only arrivals to reach them were persons who had demonstrated the firmest sort of sales resistance, the drivers in the free spaces recognized the necessity for extreme measures.

Some of them wrestled the arrivals for their luggage. One woman driver near Bob kept shouting, "See Nantucket with a gal." Another woman alleged that she—meaning of course her cab, because there really isn't any of that other kind of business in Nantucket—had the lowest rates in town. Bob, who couldn't bring himself to wrestle for luggage and who felt silly even whispering "taxi," at least had the satisfaction of noting that he wasn't any less successful than the others in the free area.

When Bob came home to Anchor Inn later that afternoon, after cruising around town for a few hours in the vain hope of picking up someone headed for the beach, he was thoroughly discouraged.

But we had to pay for the car somehow, and Bob met the steamers for the next five days. Although he soon lost his reluctance to holler "taxi" and wrestle passengers for their suitcases, his efforts resulted in only two fares, neither of which came to Anchor Inn.

On the sixth day, having been busy repairing a clogged sink on the second floor, my husband did not look his best when he drove hastily to the wharf to try his luck again. The steamer had already arrived and the passengers were filing down the wharf. Bob parked quickly in the free area, jumped out of the car shouting "taxi" and bumped blindly into a neatly dressed, conservative, elderly man and his middle-aged, plump wife.

"Taxi! Sir! Taxi!" bellowed Bob. "Take you any place on the island! Lowest rates! Taxi! Taxi!"

"No thank you," said the elderly gentleman, probably for the fiftieth time since he had stepped off the steamer. "We prefer . . . Why, it's Robert Gilbreth, isn't it?"

Bob looked again at the face of the reluctant fare and discovered that it belonged to a high-ranking executive of the firm for which

Bob had worked in New York. It was not a very pleasant experience for either of them.

"Good to see you, Mr. Gilbreth," said the executive with a great show of heartiness. "Well, this *is* a surprise. Yes, indeed! It's Robert Gilbreth, dear."

"Who?" said his wife, looking without approval at Bob's greasy blue jeans and soiled workshirt.

"Robert Gilbreth," said the executive, who was going to be democratic if it killed him. "I used to know him in New York."

"How do you do, Mr. Gilbreth," his wife said.

"Hi," gulped Bob. "It's nice to see you, Mr. Booker. How do you do, Mrs. Booker. Er, welcome to Nantucket."

"Mr. Gilbreth used to be with us in personnel," explained Mr. Booker.

Mrs. Booker studied Bob again. She looked at the taxi sign on the station wagon.

"I see," she said, and her voice indicated that Bob had probably been fired for drinking on the job and now had come to the end of a wretched trail, driving a taxicab for somebody else on an outpost in the Atlantic. "Well, it was nice seeing you, Mr. Gilbreth," she added. "Come along, William!"

"It was nice seeing you," Mr. Booker echoed. "I hope we'll see you around some time."

They started to edge away. Bob striving desperately to appear at ease, advised: "I wouldn't walk too far in the sun, if I were you. It's deceiving, because it doesn't feel very hot. But it will certainly give you a burn."

"Indeed?" inquired Mrs. Booker, apparently interpreting Bob's remarks as a final plea from a down-and-outer who had reached the point where he would beg former acquaintances for their patronage.

"Perhaps we'd better take Mr. Gilbreth's taxi after all," Mr. Booker relented. "He's right. That sun is bearing down."

"I didn't mean *that*," blushed Bob.

"Quite all right," said Mr. Booker.

They got in the back and asked Bob to drive them to the Nantucket Information Bureau.

"We thought perhaps the bureau could tell us where to find a quiet inn, with Colonial atmosphere," Mr. Booker explained. "You wouldn't know of any such place, would you?"

What they were looking for pretty well fitted the description of Anchor Inn. Although we certainly could have used two more guests, Bob decided he wasn't going to give Mrs. Booker the opportunity of considering him a tout for his own flophouse.

"I think we'd better ask at the information bureau," she put in firmly.

"I'm sure that's best," agreed Bob.

Bob parked near the Dreamland Theater and waited while they went into the information bureau. They returned a few minutes later, laden with "literature" and a list of five or six inns which might meet their specifications. Mrs. Booker read off the names, and asked Bob if he knew where they were.

"Yes, ma'am," said Bob. "Which one do you want to try first?"

"The closest one."

"They're all about the same distance," Bob replied quite truthfully. "Suppose I take them alphabetically, so I can keep track of them better. Didn't one of them start with an 'A'?"

"Anchor Inn," Mrs. Booker nodded.

Bob drove them to our place without further comment, and as he pulled up at the curb Mrs. Booker decided that Anchor Inn was "precious."

"Do you want me to wait while you look it over, in case you

don't like it and want to try the next place on the list?" Bob asked.

"That won't be necessary," said Mrs. Booker, declining this obvious bid for additional taxi service. "I'm sure we'll like it. Pay the man, dear."

She walked up our front steps, leaving her husband with the obviously embarrassing decision of whether he should offer Bob a tip.

"How much is that, Mr. Gilbreth?" he inquired.

"It's a dollar," Bob told him. "But we'll add it to your bill when you check out."

Although I tactfully refrained from saying it in so many words, I had a definite impression that Bob could do a great deal better as a taxi driver if he were more aggressive in seeking passengers. I kept dropping hints to this effect, when he came home empty-handed and discouraged after meeting the steamers. The hints finally got under Bob's skin, and led to one of the few really great debates we had had about the operation of our business enterprises.

The specific hint which touched off the debate was an innocent observation by me about the headgear worn by many of the cab drivers. Some cabbies wore chauffeurs' caps with "taxi" signs above the hard visors, and others wore yachting caps and affected the sea-captain look. Competition was so keen that several of the taxi skippers had donned enough additional gold braid and "scrambled eggs" to promote themselves to commodores and even chiefs of naval operations. Two of the most successful cab operators, both bearing the same surname, were distinguished from each other by their titles. They were known as Cap'n Folger and Admiral Folger. "And I suppose," snapped Bob, "that you think I ought to wear a cap with either five stars or 'taxi' on it. If you had your way,

I'd get *two* signs and walk around like a sandwich man advertising the inn."

"I didn't say anything about a sandwich man," I protested. "I simply pointed out that some cab drivers think those caps are a good idea."

"And what you're getting at, by your usually devious route," said my husband, "is that I should buy myself such a cap. Why don't you come right out and say so? You want me to wear one of those ridiculous, asinine caps with 'taxi' on it. Go ahead. Admit it."

"All right," I hollered. "I admit it. Go get one, and then maybe you'll get some *passengers*."

"That," enunciated Bob, "does it."

"What do you mean, that does it?"

"I mean I resign as cab driver," said Bob, hollering too. "I quit! Let the finance company have the station wagon. Taxiing is a waste of time and a waste of gasoline."

"Go ahead and be a quitter then," I tried to shame him. "Go ahead and be discouraged because of a few minor reverses."

"A few minor reverses?" yelped Bob indignantly. "I've had enough reverses to diagram next year's plays for the whole Notre Dame football schedule."

"You mean you've had enough errors," I put in. "You've dropped the ball, that's what you've done."

"Simply because you have hopelessly lost your temper," Bob asserted precisely, in the maddeningly reasonable tone which he sometimes adopts after he has lost *his,* "there is no no need to scream like a fishwife or carelessly to mix metaphors. If you are employing the analogy of football, it would be fumbles, not errors."

"Errors or fumbles," I megaphoned, "you've *had* them, brother. You've had them ever since you got behind the wheel of that station wagon."

Bob forgot his reasonable tone. If I had been a fishwife, he **was** now being a fishmonger.

"Every day," he informed the neighbors, our guests, and me, "I go down to the steamer while the other drivers look at me as if I were taking bread out of their children's mouths. Every day I go out on the dock and scream 'taxi,' while hoping I won't run into any of my old friends of the yacht club crowd, let alone my own brothers and sisters. And while I'm hellishly screaming 'taxi,' I'm in there wrestling for suitcases like a street urchin scrambling for pennies. And now you have the colossal, insolent brass to suggest that I'm not trying to get fares, and that I additionally should perch upon my head one of those miserable little caps as the final badge of my degradation. To hell with it!"

"In other words, you won't do it," I summed it up.

"In other words, to hell with it. I quit!"

"Then tomorrow," I informed him, "*you* can cook all the breakfasts, *you* can make all the beds, *you* can vacuum all the rooms, *you* can clean out all the tubs, *you* can wash out all the johns, *you* . . ."

"It will be my pleasure," interrupted Bob, bowing gallantly. "And you, I take it, will be driving the taxi?"

"Exactly," I said.

"Might I inquire," said Bob, now the perfect gentleman again, "as to your head size? Before I assume my duties as cook and chambermaid, I thought I might wander up town and buy you a little cap."

"Don't bother," I replied. "I'll get fares without a cap, you'll see." I headed for the bedroom, and slammed the door. But I couldn't resist opening it again long enough to stick out my head and add what should have been my exit line. "Besides," I hollered, "what would you use for *money?*"

I slammed the door again.

Bob and I didn't have any more unpleasant words—or, in fact, any words at all—for the remainder of the day. The one remark which he wished to address to me he routed via Ann, at the supper table.

"Please tell your mother," he said, "that if she intends to resort to a pitch such as 'See Nantucket with a gal,' someone's already got a patent on it."

"Tell your father, 'Humph,'" I instructed Ann.

Two of our guests, both women, planned to leave on the six-o'clock boat the next morning. After supper I went up to their rooms to ask if they would like transportation to the dock. They both said they would. I set the alarm for five o'clock, and it was pitch dark when I crawled out of bed to begin my first day of hacking.

I loaded the women's luggage into the station wagon, drove them to the steamer, and helped them tote the luggage aboard. By the time the job was done, I had worked up a healthy perspiration and healthy appetite for breakfast.

"You and your husband provide wonderful service," one of the women told me as we shook hands on the gangplank. "I'll certainly be back next year, and I'll tell my friends about Anchor Inn, too."

"You have so many thoughtful little extras," said the second woman, nodding agreement. "For instance, it's marvelous the way you deliver the New Bedford papers, free of charge, to the rooms every afternoon."

"That's one of my husband's ideas," I beamed, because I like nothing better than hearing praise about the inn. "The papers really don't cost much, and I think they've brought us a lot of good will."

"Of course they have," the second woman continued. "And finally there is this last act of graciousness—getting up before dawn and taking your guests down to the steamer in your own car, to bid them goodbye. It makes me feel as if I were one of the family."

"Thank you for everything, dear," said the first woman, pecking me on the cheek.

They waved and walked up the gangplank. Since they considered themselves members of the family—and kissing kin at that—I didn't have the heart to bellow at them that this final service was not meant to be gratis. I'm sure they weren't trying to beat me out of anything. It was simply that it never occurred to them, I guess, that I'd be driving a taxi in my spare time.

Even though I didn't collect any money, the sunrise was worth my trip to the dock. Anyone who writes a book about an island should be entitled to describe at least five sunrises. I haven't used up my quota yet.

This was a special one. There wasn't any hope of finding a fare until people were up and stirring, so I climbed to the top of a piling at the end of the wharf and watched the sky come to life.

The steamer hustled away in a cloud of phosphorescent dust. She was out of sight around Brant Point when the sun fire-balled through the gunmetal haze over Coatue, the eastern prong of Nantucket's horseshoe. A fleet of small, commercial fishing boats, edged crabwise away from their berths and pointed their bows at the fiery explosion. They single-filed bravely toward the continental shelf, while a squadron of gulls flew protective cover.

When I went back to Anchor Inn for breakfast, the soul-lifting experience of the sunrise was almost—but not quite—enough to make me forget that I was still furious with Bob.

He and Ann had already eaten. Bob, wearing one of my ruffled aprons, was fixing fried eggs for early-rising guests. I might have forgiven him if he had acted as if my daily duties—which he was now assuming—were arduous or harrowing. Instead, he was going out of his way to prove that a person with normal intelligence could perform all these household chores with leisurely ease.

It has long been a source of annoyance to me that, although I have fried tens of thousands of eggs, compared with Bob's hundreds, his whites are always snowy and firm, whereas mine are gray and gooshy or brown and leathery. Also, almost as often as not, I accidentally break the yolks.

Ordinarily in the summers, our own breakfasts are composed of eggs I've ruined, while cooking for the guests. Bob and Ann, sitting around the kitchen table, would eat the broken-yolk "rejects," and when Bob and Ann were full, I'd eat them myself. Sometimes, after I was full, there'd even be enough of the "rejects" to put in the icebox and save for lunch.

So now I sat down silently in Bob's place at the table, and waited patiently for the "rejects." Bob is normally the fancy Dan kind of cook—a frustrated griddle-cake counterman, I guess—who is inclined to flip up things into the air, to toss grease into a frying pan as if he were having a butter-ball fight, and to break open eggs with one hand. That morning, he outdid himself.

He not only broke the eggs into the frying pan with one hand, but also added insult to injury by using the other hand to hold a magazine, which he pretended to be nonchalantly reading. When the eggs were done, he'd put down the magazine long enough to grab a plate. Then he'd toss the eggs, in a high spinning parabola, onto the plate. He never missed or punctured the yolks, although sometimes he would have to dash halfway across the room to make the catch, and there were a couple of grease marks on the ceiling testifying to his ability to play them off the walls, as well as nail them on the fly. I did my best to ignore these antics, although of course Ann was an enthusiastic audience.

When the guests had been taken care of, and there were still no "rejects," Bob fried a couple of eggs especially for me. I like them over light, as he knows, and this gave him an opportunity for two flips. The latter of these, a grand finale, involved a sweeping, shoe-string catch just a split second before the eggs splashed on the floor.

"You think you're pretty smart, don't you?" I inquired, breaking the silence.

But Bob, now washing dishes with one hand, apparently was too occupied with his magazine to answer.

I ate the eggs and they were perfect.

"How were they?" Bob finally couldn't resist asking.

"There wasn't anything wrong with them," I admitted cautiously.

"Well, how about it?" he added. "Was it worth a dollar to get up at five o'clock and rush those two gals down to the steamer? Tell the truth now. It wasn't worth it, was it?"

"Oh, I guess it was," I hedged. I had intended to tell him about my not being paid but, in view of his attitude, I decided to postpone that confession—perhaps indefinitely. I was confident I could make up the money, through other fares, later in the day.

I spent all morning, either cruising or parked at a curb. A certain amount of curb space is reserved for taxis, but these stands were almost invariably full. When I'd park in a space not specifically reserved for cabs, an alert town policeman would tell me to move along. After the third such warning, he said he wasn't going to tell me again. But he did.

I finally found a space at a taxi stand near the old, three-story Pacific Club, one of Nantucket's skyscrapers, at the foot of Main Street. The club was once the social center and story-swapping headquarters of the whaling captains. Having nothing better to do, I read and re-read signs on the outside wall about the Nantucket ships *Dartmouth, Beaver* and *Eleanor*. As all islanders know, the Pacific Club is the place where the skippers of the "Datmuth, Beevuh and Elner" received orders from a merchant in 1773 to take a cargo of whale oil to England and return to Boston with a cargo of tea. At anchor in Boston, the three ships played host to a group of "wild Indians" at the Boston Tea Party. Today the Pacific Club is the town's cribbage center, and the tourist publications *This Week in Nantucket* and *Nantucket Holiday* announce proudly that the club's members are "ready to take on anyone." Thus it cannot be said that the spirit of derring-do has completely vanished from the island.

By lunchtime, I still hadn't gotten a single fare. When I went home to eat, I found that Bob was just finishing the job of cleaning the rooms. I had sometimes complained of an aching back from leaning over to vacuum under the beds. Bob had solved this problem—again, obviously, for my benefit—by bringing up Ann's express wagon to accommodate himself and the tank of the vacuum cleaner. He had rigged the express wagon with the back of a beach chair, against which he was lounging luxuriously, and seemed to enjoy propelling himself around the various rooms.

"If we hadn't thrown away the old ironer," he informed me, "I'll bet I could rig a motor for this thing."

Since he had cleaned the rooms immaculately and was well ahead of my schedule, I couldn't very well complain.

After a quick lunch, I dashed down to meet the steamer. I had honestly intended to take the taxi sign off the windshield, elbow my way right up to the gangplank, and stand there holding the sign over my head and hollering "taxi," as the passengers debarked. But when the chips were down and I was confronted by the well-dressed and dignified crowd of summer people meeting the boat, I simply couldn't make myself do it. Of course I didn't get a fare.

See Nantucket with a Gal

I had already planned my method of procedure, if I failed to pick up any passengers at the boat. While the cabs from the rented spaces were delivering their fares, I'd tool out to the Nantucket Memorial Airport and get at the front of the taxi line to meet the Boston plane.

I careened away from the dock and, ignoring the speed laws, headed out of town. As I passed Our Island Home, the institution for the needy old people, I couldn't help thinking of Bob's frequent and dire warnings that it will be the ultimate destination for both of us, if we don't pay off the mortgage on the inn. Keeping the accelerator down to the floorboards, I took the new hard-surfaced shortcut through a rolling, miniature forest of wind-dwarfed pine, and banked into the airport entrance just as the Northeast Airlines plane from Boston was landing.

I had heard reports that there once were mysterious tunnels, a part of the "underground railroad" for runaway slaves, from the dock sections into town. I still don't believe those reports, but I *did* see in the airport taxi line, well ahead of me, ten or twelve cabs which had still been on the steamer wharf when I left. How they beat me out there, without using tunnels, remains a mystery.

Under the airport rules, cabs had to cue up and wait their turns. Soliciting of fares wasn't allowed. If you stayed in the line long enough, you were certain to get a fare.

However, almost everyone on the Boston plane was met by friends. Only the two cabs at the head of the line got passengers. A plane from New York—the last until after dark—was scheduled to arrive in fifteen minutes. It was late, and I waited patiently while the clock scissored off an hour and five minutes. Again, only two taxis got fares. I had moved up four places in line, but there were still about eight cabs ahead of me, not to mention five in back of me.

The driver immediately behind me, a middle-aged man with

rumpled clothes, got out to stretch his legs and came wandering up to the station wagon to make conversation.

"Too bad the Red Sox ain't playin' this afternoon," he allowed. "It ain't so bad waitin' when the Red Sox is playin'."

I'm not a baseball fan, but in order to maintain intelligently your end of the conversation with a Nantucketer, it is necessary to keep up with the activities of the Boston team. The sports page of the Boston *Post* had long since become required reading for me.

"They're going against Cleveland tonight," I nodded. "Parnell and Feller."

"Ain't yer Mrs. Anchor?" he asked, offering me a cigarette.

I said I was, and took the cigarette.

"Yer gonna wait for the night plane?"

"I don't know. I'm so far back in the line it looks as if I wouldn't get a passenger then, either."

"Yer might get one by morning, though," he said encouragingly.

"You mean stay here all night?"

"There's plenty of us that do. We got to have something to show for the twenty-five dollars that the airport charges for parkin' in this line."

"Twenty-five dollars!" I gasped. "You mean there's a season rental fee for parking in this line?"

"Sure is. Yer ain't paid it yet? The man that collects it is around here someplace."

"I'm sure my husband's paid it," I lied.

"That's good, because the man that collects it usually comes around every hour or so, to check up."

"You know," I said brightly, "I don't think I'll wait for the night plane after all. I wonder if you'd mind backing your car up a little and letting me out?"

"Yer got to be patient in this business," he reproved me.

"I really do have to be going," I told him, looking to make certain that the collections man wasn't approaching.

"Okay," he nodded. "Sure, I'll back up."

I got away from there fast. But I found out later that, unlike the steamer dock, no rent was charged for taxis at the airport. I guess that friendly driver had made up the story, so as to get my place in line.

Now, I decided to return to town by the Nobadeer road, which connects with the highway to Siasconset, a former fishing village which became a summer colony for noted actors in the Nineties. Its name has been shortened to Sconset by the economical Nantucketers, and it is now a fashionable and unbelievably beautiful resort, with the weather-beaten fishing shacks covered with rambling roses that climb over the roofs and chimneys.

I didn't run into any fares on the Sconset road, although a number of people were out walking. Giving up in disgust, I returned to Anchor Inn.

There I found a note from Bob saying that, having finished his work and mine, he had taken Ann to the beach for the afternoon. It was the first time any of us had found an opportunity to get to the beach that summer. Although there wasn't anything to be done at the inn until suppertime, I was mad enough to shoot him.

It took me about forty-five seconds to get into my bathing suit, and about fifteen seconds to stalk angrily out to the car, with a towel around my shoulders. It was so warm that I didn't even bother with a beach robe.

As I was about to pull away from the curb, two middle-aged men in outlandish sport clothes waddled by, noted the taxi sign, looked me over with what I hopefully believe was approval, and nudged each other.

"Hello, beautiful," said one, grinning obscenely and tipping

183

the foot-long, plastic bill of a cap which, if he only knew it, made him look like a pelican on the prowl. "Do all lady cab drivers on Nantucket work in bathing suits?"

"Shove off, Mac," I ordered. "I'm going to the beach."

"Well, that's a jolly coincidence," he leered. "She knows my name and she's going the same place we're going. Hop in, Carl."

"After you, 'Mac,'" bowed Carl, who also had a cap with a foot-long bill. "And ask her if she's got a friend."

"In the back, penguins," I pointed. "That is, if you really want to go to the beach. The charge will be one dollar and I haven't got a friend in the world—and don't want to make any new ones."

They got in the back, and Carl handed me a dollar.

"Don't you think you could find me a friend at the beach?" he asked.

"Not a chance," I replied firmly. "I'm meeting my husband there, and believe me, he's no friend of mine. And I don't think he will like you very well, either."

I started driving toward the beach, and the penguins rubbed bills as they held a whispered huddle.

"On second thought," "Mac" announced, "we believe we'll stroll around town for awhile. Would you mind letting us out here?"

"The charge for that short ride," I snapped, stopping the car, "is fifteen cents. I owe you eighty-five."

"Keep the chicken feed, honey-chile," said Carl. "If you change your mind, we'll be around."

As I drove alone to the beach, I figured that, at any rate, I now had the dollar I should have collected from the two guests who hadn't known they were supposed to pay.

I finally found Bob, lying half asleep on a public beach near The Shoe, while Ann played at the edge of the water. Since there

wasn't any work to be done at the inn, I couldn't find anything
with which to reproach him. But, just the same, I was in what our
friend Mrs. Macy describes as an ugly pet.

"Quitting so soon," Bob applied the gentle needle. "You can't
get any customers if you're going to loll around in a bathing suit,
you know."

"That's what *you* think," I muttered.

"You're not going to miss the night boat and the night plane,
are you?"

"Just leave me alone!" I demanded.

I stretched out alongside of him, and the sun felt warm and good.

"Have you been in yet?" I asked Bob sleepily.

"Twice. It's a little chilly going in, but it's wonderful when you
get wet."

"I'd like to lie here forever," I groaned, almost forgetting that I
was furious with him. Then, recalling my painful efforts at cab
driving while he basked idly on the beach, I had an ugly thought.

"Since I had the car," I asked suspiciously, sitting up in the sand,
"how did you and Ann get to the beach?"

"How would we get here?" Bob yawned. "We took a cab, naturally."

I grabbed the first thing I could find, which happened to be a
handful of sand, and threw it at him.

"Hey, cut that out!" Bob yelped.

Tears were stinging my eyes, and I got some more sand and
threw it. Bob was lucky there weren't any rocks on that part of
the beach.

"Cut that out!" he hollered, trying to protect his face with his
hands.

"You dirty dog!" I hissed, hurling sand with both hands. "You

all-American louse. It's bad enough that you'd take *any* cab. But if
you had to waste the money, you might at least have taken the
cab your own *wife* was driving."

"We walked," surrendered Bob, who by then had knotted himself into a ball, with his head protectively between his knees. "I
was only joking. We walked, I tell you."

"Honest?"

"Ask Ann, if you don't believe me. And cut it out or I'll flatten
you."

Bob peeked tentatively from under a kneepit, to determine
whether it was safe to emerge. Not that I didn't believe him, but I
went down to the water's edge anyway, to check with Ann. They
had walked, all right.

I didn't hear Bob tiptoe up behind me, but the next thing I knew
he had picked me up and dived with me into the icy water. I came
to the surface gasping and blowing water out of my nose.

"That," said Bob, putting arm around my waist and pulling me
close to him, "is for throwing sand at me. Next time I'll *drown*
you!"

We walked out together toward the diving raft. Bob was right.
The water was wonderful, once you got in.

Thereafter, we retired from the taxi business, except to cater to
our own guests and Mrs. Macy's. We put up a sign on our own
bulletin board, and she let us put a similar sign up on hers, saying
that the station wagon was available "FOR A FEE" to take
guests to the steamer and the airport, and to the South Shore for
surf picnics. We made enough money to meet the payments on
the car during the summer months. During the winter, the payments simply had to be absorbed in our budget.

13 ～ Innside Etiquette

By the middle week of July in that second summer, Anchor Inn
was overflowing again and we were booked almost solidly until
Labor Day. Bob and I were so busy that we couldn't have gone out
to solicit taxi fares even if we had wanted to. Extra rent from the
attic rooms enabled us to hire a school girl to help with the chambermaid's duties.

Ann, now slightly more than two years old, seldom cried any
more at night. She was still, however, far from an asset to the inn
business.

Having seen me require guests to register, she got in the habit of
registering herself whenever we weren't looking. Sometimes she
registered in pen and ink, sometimes in pencil, and sometimes in
colored crayon. When I caught her in the act, I could take a razor
blade and cut out of the registry the sheet she had decorated. But
many a guest, on being asked by me to sign his name as required

by law, found that the place where he was supposed to write contained ink smudges, crosses, and Ann's versions of sailboats, horsies, whales and Sandy Claws coming down the chimney.

In addition to decorating the registry, our daughter also enjoyed providing music for the entertainment of our guests. One of her prized possessions was a hurdy-gurdy type of music box which hung from a shoulder strap and which played "God Bless America" when she turned the crank. Ann usually sang to the music box's accompaniment but, since she preferred "Away in a Manger" to "God Bless America," her concerts were seldom harmonious.

Unluckily, an organ grinder and his monkey arrived on the island for a couple of weeks that summer, and Ann was immediately impressed by the similarity between his hurdy-gurdy and hers.

A couple of days later, one of the children in the neighborhood came running into the kitchen to inform me that Ann was begging in the street. I went out there and found that she was sitting on our front steps, ringed by a dozen or so amused passersby. She was cranking her hurdy-gurdy and singing "Away in a Manger." Along side of her on the steps was another of her prized possessions—a motheaten toy panda which for the moment had been impressed into service as a monkey—and my aluminum measuring cup. The cup was about half full of pennies and nickels.

Also, no matter how firm our discipline, we couldn't completely break our daughter of the habit of making the rounds upstairs to pay social calls on the guests. Since some of them spoiled her with candy and other presents, she naturally assumed she was welcome. I'm afraid she also assumed that, when I went up to clean the rooms, I, too, was showered with presents and stuffed with candy; and that my objection to her making the rounds stemmed from a selfish desire to keep anyone from muscling in on my delightful racket.

Of course, Ann never bothered to knock when she went visiting and never bothered to close doors behind her. This oversight possibly annoyed and embarrassed some of our guests, particularly those who were not accustomed to entertaining young ladies in their rooms. I *know* it annoyed and embarrassed Bob and me.

Ann enjoyed getting presents so much that she went through a distressing period of giving presents, too. The gifts she bestowed on our guests were usually wrapped thoroughly, if not daintily, in brown paper bags which had contained our groceries. Occasionally, in what must have been a dim recollection of the preceding Christmas, she'd slip two or three presents, unwrapped, into one of my nylons, and then give away the stocking.

The presents themselves ran the gamut of Bob's and my belongings, from our toothbrushes to (once) a diary that I had kept for a few months, and from our soiled handkerchiefs to (twice) Bob's wallet. The guests would make a great to-do over the child when she gave them the gifts, unwrapping the objects with amazement that wasn't always feigned, thanking her profusely, and alleging solemnly that the gifts were *just* what they'd always wanted. This served merely to inspire Ann to new heights of kleptomania, from our meager stock of worldly goods.

Of course, the guests would later return the presents to us, when Ann wasn't around—unless the gifts happened to be in the category of empty ginger ale bottles or empty cans of beans, which could be thrown away. But it got to a point where I could hardly drop a piece of facial tissue in the wastebasket before Ann would have it either gift-wrapped in a paper bag or wadded into the toe of a stocking.

I never could make out for sure whether the presents Ann gave were designed to attract gifts to herself, as in casting bread on the waters, or whether they were motivated by a sincere belief that it was better to give than to receive. Since I am her mother, I am naturally inclined to subscribe to the latter theory.

Once, when Ann called on a honeymooning couple to deliver a paper bag which still smelled of onions and which contained a stack of canceled checks I had just received from the bank, she found that her hosts weren't at home. Deciding to wait for them, she soon noticed that the bride's cosmetics were spread out on a bureau.

Ann knew very well she wasn't allowed even so much as to touch my cosmetics. But again she may have figured that I was just naturally selfish about such matters, whereas the bride, who had been especially nice to her, wouldn't object at all to sharing a minute portion of the make-up materials which she possessed in such fascinating abundance.

After putting on enough creams, lotions, powders, perfumes, and paints to attend a ceremony at which a missionary was to be barbecued, Ann dressed herself in the bride's finery. This included high-heeled pumps, an evening dress of tulle over aqua taffeta, and a girdle which Ann wore over both the tulle *and* taffeta.

Proud of her appearance, she stumbled safely down the stairs without being thrown by the pumps or tripped by the girdle's garters. I found her in the lobby where, presumably, she intended to register in her new identity. She seemed surprised and disappointed that I recognized her.

Fortunately, no one was in the lobby and I was able to repair the damage and retrieve my canceled checks before the honeymooners returned. After that, we put Ann in a summer kindergarten—a play school where she could spend most of the day at the beach and we could go about our work without having to watch her.

Innside Etiquette

In many respects, honeymooners are the most desirable of all guests. They're not demanding, they stay out of the way, they're considerate of each other, they're quiet, and they're so happy that it's nice to have them around. The only drawback to honeymooners is that they are seldom "repeaters"—in other words, you won't see them again in subsequent summers. The reason is that usually they are young and the bridegroom is just starting out in business. They can well afford a place like Anchor Inn for their wedding trip, but not for annual vacations. Besides, children will be coming along and the young parents will be tied down.

Mrs. Macy says that honeymooners sometimes come back fifteen or twenty years later, on a sentimental journey. Then, if they still like the inn, they may become "repeaters." Congenial "repeaters" can be an inn's best asset.

An inn's worst asset undoubtedly are the flashy, ill-mannered, loud-talking, uncultured, boorish phonies who think that by exhibiting large quantities of unadulterated crust they will be mistaken for members of the upper crust. They are the ones who wave currency of large denominations; who effect a broad "a" as they mouth their cliches and inanities; and who holler "boy" at Bob when they summon him regally for innumerable errands.

They discover, almost immediately, that every Anchor Inn accommodation is primitively inferior to the gracious living at their own homes—homes, which, one gathers, are the latest thing in luxurious mansions, and are overflowing with uniformed flunkies.

They monopolize the lobby, shout at each other from room to room and tie up the bathrooms by doing huge quantities of personal laundry there. At the risk of being considered snobbish myself, I will embrace—but only figuratively, you can bet your boots— these worst assets of an inn under the generic term of peasants, in the urban sense of the word.

Actually, many real members of the so-called upper crust journey to Nantucket for the summers, but not many of them come to Anchor Inn. Most of them have their own homes on Millionaires Row, up on the Cliff. Some of them live aboard their yachts. A few of them get suites at the Gordon Folger Hotel, which old-timers will remember as the Point Breeze.

We cater, as I've pointed out, to conservative, middle-income people: business girls, wedding trippers, suburbanites with one or two children, teachers, junior executives who some day may move up to Millionaires Row, progressive farmers, couples living on retirement pensions, widows. If that sounds like a stuffy group, it shouldn't; because I'm talking pretty much about the "average" moderately well-off American on his two-week vacation. Almost all of these people—representing different age groups, different parts of the country, different religions, and different national origins—seem instinctively to have good manners and to show thoughtful consideration for inn operators and fellow guests.

As to the others—the "urban peasants"—someone should write for them a special book of etiquette about behavior at a quiet resort inn. Since no one has done so, I propose to list here a few things which guests should avoid, especially if they don't want Bob to toss them out of Anchor Inn.

Item: Most inn proprietors expect their guests to do a certain amount of light laundry, and do not object to the practice. It is quite true that clothes will dry rapidly if suspended in the frame of an open window. But it is equally true that such suspension does not enhance the appearance of an inn, when seen from the street. Frankly, it makes a handsome old inn resemble an ugly old tenement, and repels potential guests who are looking for a place to stay.

Innside Etiquette

We have had guests who hung laundry outside their windows, and then asked for some sort of an adjustment because traces of the house paint rubbed off on their clothes. Also, we had one woman who did all of her own and her husband's laundry every day, placed the wash on clothes hangers, hooked the hangers onto a closed umbrella, and extended the umbrella flag-pole-fashion from a third-story window.

I handle the inveterate window-driers by suggesting that their laundry and bathing suits would dry even faster if they would use the clothes lines in our back yard. If they don't get the hint, Bob takes over and tells them with his customary subtlety that we are neither operating a slum nor trying to run out of business any commercial laundries.

Item: Men who chainsmoke cigars either in their bedrooms or in share-the-baths should occasionally open the windows.

Item: Wet bathing suits and spilled whisky are ruinous to the finish of antique furniture. When anything is spilled on a dresser, it should be promptly wiped up. To slide a dresser scarf over the liquid doesn't fool anyone, and additionally causes the scarf to stick to the varnish.

Item: If inn proprietors wanted little brass hooks to be screwed into closet doors and the headboards of beds—to hold such items as special reading lamps, clocks, barometers, and calendars—the proprietors would have furnished these hooks.

A guest thus can safely take it for granted, when there isn't already a hook in a specific place, that the management doesn't desire a hook there.

If I had my way, customs men would be stationed at the wharfs and airport to examine the luggage of visitors for these screw-in hooks. And the board of selectmen would pass an ordinance forbidding local hardware stores to sell the hooks, except to those customers who can produce proof that they own property on the island.

Item: Parking bicycles, fishing poles, surf boards, and inflated life rafts against the front of an inn, so that the place resembles a display yard for second-hand goods, is seldom appreciated by the management. I've had strangers ring the front door bell and try to buy certain articles left out front by guests. And there have been a few times when I was so aggravated I felt like selling the articles on the spot.

Item: When an inn has a lobby smaller than the living room in an average home, the lobby obviously cannot comfortably accommodate twenty or thirty persons. Most guests realize this. They understand that the lobby, particularly if it is furnished with fragile and valuable antiques, exists largely for decorative purposes. They certainly might sit quietly in the lobby and read a book or entertain a friend. But if they intend to do any relaxing, drinking, or party-throwing, they should do so in their own rooms.

At Anchor Inn, the least desirable-looking guests are almost invariably the lobby hogs. If one of your "on-the-blind" reservations turns out to have sideburns down to his ear-lobes and a sheiky, pencil-line moustache; or wears jeweled bracelets on her ankles and heavy bluing shadow on her eyelids, you may well have a lobby hog.

The lobby hogs always talk in loud voices, wear extreme clothes, and get raucous on the second drink after leaving rings from glasses on the furniture.

I do not object in the slightest to this when done elsewhere. In fact I can get raucous on the *first* drink. But not in my inn, and, especially not in my lobby. It hurts business.

"Refined" may be a stodgy word, but it's surprising how many of our guests, writing for reservations, want to be certain that we're operating that sort of an inn.

We have lost potential guests, looking for refinement, who have entered our front door while lobby hogs were making a pigpen of the place.

It's Bob's job to give the heave to the lobby hogs. I can't walk up to a flashy number and tell her that unless she takes off half of her pancake makeup and half of her costume jewelry, and then puts on twice as many clothes, she's liable to ruin our business. And I can't inform a sleek male charmer with a tango haircut that it would be all right for him to frequent the lobby if he'd lower his voice, shorten his watch chain and his sideburns and cut eight inches off the bottom of his sport coat. Of course it would help if he would also throw away the artificial nosegay in his lapel and do something about his yellow, suede shoes, but an inn proprietor can't expect *everything*.

Bob can't tell them that, in just so many words, either. But he has other effective ways, usually thought up on the spur of the moment, of dealing with such nuisances.

Once, for instance, Bob watched with increasing fury a noisy, alcoholic bridge game, complete with kibitzers, in the lobby. At the beginning of the game, it had been "Boy, get some ice" and "Boy, get some glasses." They had kept the bottle under the table, at first, but finally they plunked it down on our most valuable piece of furniture—the applewood desk. Cigarettes were being stamped out on our antique floorboards.

"Boy," called one of the players, flipping a dollar bill at Bob, "more ice."

Bob walked murderously into the room, picked up the bottle by its neck, and walked over to the man who had flipped him the dollar.

"Just once," Bob demanded, "I want to hear you say 'please.' "

"Please," stuttered the man, keeping a wary eye on the bottle. "You can't get away with that—threatening your guests with a bottle."

"I'm not threatening you with it," declared Bob. "I'm just getting it off my desk. And now the whole bunch of you clear out of the lobby and stay out of the lobby."

It did seem to me that, if Bob's only purpose in picking up the bottle was to get it off the desk, there wasn't any need for him to be swinging it in circles above his head.

However, the exodus was satisfactorily general, and Bob soon recovered his temper sufficiently to follow them out of the lobby and *hand* them back the bottle.

They were holding a whispered council of war in the front hall, and one of the women told Bob that they had a good mind to check out of Anchor Inn that very night.

"Modom," said Bob, now falling back on the dignified half-whisper he had plagiarized from Mrs. Macy, "I am gratified to observe your sensitivity to a hint, however slight."

They didn't check out, though. The surest way to keep some guests is to intimate that you'd like them to leave.

14~ The Rumor Mill

Having lived in several small New England towns, I am familiar with the workings of rumor mills.

Most such mills chew up and disgorge the grist of gossip, speculation and party-line eaves-dropping. The Nantucketers' rumor mill, while not ignoring any of these three valuable sources, draws its principal raw material from shrewd deduction. True enough, reports sometimes are exaggerated, as the case of the Bob Gilbreths' prosperity. But for speed and overall accuracy, I believe the Nantucket mill compares favorably with any in the world. In this generalization, I do not exclude those tropical countries where the natives pass along, via tom toms, choice tidbits about intrepid explorer-authors who, to hear them tell it, are in constant danger of themselves becoming choice tidbits.

To a summer resident, the deductions of Nantucketers not only seem shrewd but sometimes supernaturally so. Actually, there's a logical explanation for most of them.

For instance, a man at a filling station told me, early one afternoon, that a good friend of Bob's and mine had just arrived on the steamer for his summer vacation. A couple of minutes later, I happened to drive down the steamer dock on an errand. I was flabbergasted to see the very same friend descend the gangplank of the boat, which had only that moment tied up.

Months later, when I better understood the functionings of the rumor mill, I asked the filling-station man about his deduction. Like most magic, the explanation was involved and caused the trick itself to sound flat.

To understand the explanation, you have to know something about the Wharf Rat Club, the most exclusive organization on the island. It is composed of a number of salty Nantucketers and congenial and boat-minded summer residents. The club's custodian and unofficial commodore is an old sea captain who runs a fishing supply store out on the Old North Wharf. The club is the store itself and an adjoining piazza which sits out over the water. The place lacks a woman's touch, which seems to suit the members. Its walls are decorated with pictures of deceased members, pictures of sailing ships, and various fishing momentoes. Cigarettes, candy, snuff, and chewing tobacco are for sale.

The organization has no dues and no formal officers. It doesn't have a formal waiting list of prospective members, either, although there are scores of summer residents and yachtsmen—including some socially prominent millionaires—who have been hanging around the waterfront for years, hoping to be tapped. I've heard that the membership is limited to a hundred, and that someone has to die before a new member can be admitted.

As a general rule, some fifteen or twenty summers of this hanging around and sailing around are requisites for off-island membership. But serving such an apprenticeship is no *guarantee* of membership, and indeed the large majority of the would-be neophites go to their graves untapped. At the opposite end of the scale, I understand that one summer visitor, who apparently had nothing special to recommend him, was taken into the club on his third trip to the wharf.

On those infrequent occasions when a new member is admitted, there is a minimum amount of ceremony. The old sea captain merely makes up his mind about someone and announces gruffly, in an off-hand manner: "All right. You're a member of the Wharf Rat Club."

Persons belonging to the club are entitled to lounging privileges and to a one-gun salute whenever they arrive at the island on the steamer. The salute is fired from the club's cannon as the vessel approaches her dock. Most passengers probably don't realize that the cannon shot actually is a salute honoring one of their number. But the salute is greatly treasured by the Wharf Rats themselves. Usually they drop the commodore a note, in advance, telling him when they'll arrive, so that the honors won't be overlooked.

Getting back to this friend of ours, he happened to be a Wharf Rat. He had written ahead for his salute. The filling-station attendant thus got word of his expected arrival. Hearing a cannon shot, the attendant had deduced that our friend was aboard the steamer, had been identified through binoculars by fellow Wharf Rats, and had been duly extended his honors.

That still doesn't explain how, a good while after that, all Nantucket seemed to be aware that I was expecting my second child, before either my doctor or I were sure and before Bob even suspected.

"I just got the straight dope up town that I'm the father of an eight-pound baby boy," Bob told me after he had bumped into that rumor. "Congratulations, honey, and where have you got him hidden?"

It also doesn't explain how the grapevine, on another occasion, carried a firm report that a certain islander had inherited a tidy sum from a Boston uncle, whereas the uncle didn't die until almost a month later. The actual death, together with the facts about the inheritance, was promptly recorded in the Nantucket newspapers. The reaction around town to the writeups was that the editors had been mighty slow in getting the word.

Nantucketers read their two weeklies avidly, but more for confirmation than for news. Readers also are curious to see whether the editors will print something that everyone knows is true, but no one will admit.

I certainly don't give the rumor mill credit for supernatural powers. I'm bound to confess, though, that if I ever heard a report on Nantucket that I was dead, I'd send for the minister.

At about the same time that I was having trouble with Ann because she was giving presents to our guests, Bob and I picked up separate rumors, both of which radically affected our way of life.

I picked up my news from the Nantucket high-school girl who was helping me do the chambermaid work. She had heard that her social science teacher had submitted his resignation to accept a better-paying industrial job on the mainland.

Meanwhile, Bob had been up town, where a clerk at Coffin's Hardware Store asked him when work was going to start on tearing down the Gilbreths' old summer cottage. Since we had been playing bridge with a couple of Bob's brothers at The Shoe the night before, and hadn't heard a word of any such plans from them or from Bob's mother, the news was a real surprise.

Bob rushed back to Anchor Inn to relay the rumor to me, and

The Rumor Mill

I was waiting for him eagerly to pass along the report about the social science teacher. By coincidence, Bob's training was in social studies. We had thought all along that it would be an ideal arrangement, now that he had his teaching certificate, if he could get a job at Nantucket High School. It would mean that we'd have all winter to make spare-time improvements on Anchor Inn, that we could open the inn earlier in the season and close it later, and, most important of all, that we wouldn't have to leave the island which was so close to our hearts.

After Bob and I exchanged scoops, he immediately telephoned the superintendent of schools, and applied for the teaching job.

We weren't particularly disappointed when the superintendent said that the social science teacher had not resigned. By then, we had enough faith in the grapevine to feel sure that, even if the teacher hadn't yet decided he wanted an industrial job on the mainland, he would do so, he would land the job, and he would quit the school system.

After the superintendent promised Bob that he'd be considered if the vacancy occurred, Bob telephoned The Shoe to check up on the other rumor.

"What's this," he asked his mother, "about tearing down The Shoe? The story's all over town, and I didn't hear a word about it over there last night. Don't you value my opinion on the subject?"

Bob's tone was bantering, but he didn't fool me and I doubt that he fooled his mother. I don't expect any of the Gilbreth men to admit it, but each considers himself an extremely sharp cookie when it comes to business transactions, and looks upon his mother as a babe in the business woods. The fact that she has been president of her own engineering firm ever since her husband died, when Bob was four years old, and the additional fact that she holds some twenty honorary degrees, are not deemed to have any bearing on the case.

There is considerable under-the-surface rivalry among Bob and his five brothers as to whose advice their mother will seek on various matters ranging from the purchase of a television set for her apartment to the disposal of a piece of real estate she owns in Montclair, New Jersey. To a definite but lesser extent, Bob's five sisters also have valuable suggestions on such matters.

"I may have my own inn on the island," Bob continued his telephone monolog to his mother, "but that doesn't mean that I'm not just as interested as everyone else in The Shoe."

"Of course you are, dear," replied his mother, who fortunately has a doctorate in psychology. "I haven't decided to tear down The Shoe at all. I was just talking about it with Frank and Bill at breakfast. I was hoping you and Barbara would stop by this morning so I could get your opinions about the matter."

"We'll be right over," Bob decided.

"So I can't imagine how the word got all over town," his mother said. "We haven't discussed it with anyone, or even made up our own minds. You see, a water pipe broke in the kitchen this morning, and the sewer's stopped again. And that's how we got on the subject of tearing down the place and building a new cottage."

Bob is as intrigued as I in following up what sometimes appear to be extra-sensory perception in the rumor mill. So, before he hung up, he quizzed his mother further.

"You're sure you didn't talk about it before this morning?" he asked.

"Positive, dear."

"Have any of you been down town this morning?"

"Nobody's left the house."

"Has anyone come there?"

"I don't think so. Wait a minute. The milkman, of course; he came when we were eating breakfast. And the plumber."

"Oh," said Bob, with his belief in the supernatural shattered once again.

He retained, however, his belief in the accuracy of the rumor mill. As we were driving over to The Shoe to join in the family discussion, he told me: "Mother hasn't made up her mind yet, but take it from me: The Shoe is practically dismantled and sold to the highest bidder."

I refrained from stating my considered opinion that the highest bid on The Shoe would be something like minus two hundred and fifty dollars—the charge of bringing a bulldozer and leveling the place. I have long since learned that, in matters affecting Bob's family, advice is neither solicited nor welcomed from the in-laws. Sometimes I forget this lesson, but always to my regret.

None of the Gilbreths enjoyed reaching the decision that The Shoe had to go. I myself, being in favor of slum clearance, had reached that decision the very first time I saw the place. But, frankly, I had since grown fond of it and I didn't like to see it go either.

Of course it was out of the question that the decision could definitely be reached merely by Bob, his mother, and the two brothers who happened to be on the island for their summer vacations. Although Bob's mother owns the place, she also is an expert at keeping peace within the family. Thus it was thought advisable to consult all family members, including Anne, Martha and Jane, who live on the West Coast. And, in order that they could intelligently make up their minds, it was additionally thought advisable to furnish them with complete data on the subject.

Since the Gilbreths pride themselves on efficiency, these data were compiled systematically.

Bob, Frank and Bill brought three different carpenter-contractors to the cottage, to see if there was any chance at all that it could be made weather tight and restored to its original condition. The contractors concurred in separate opinions that this was impossible.

"In the first place," one contractor explained, "it's too far gone to fix it like it used to be. And in the second place, even the way it used to be, it wasn't no good."

So that much was established, and sent in a round-robin letter to all members of the family. The Shoe couldn't be fixed.

The next step was to bring out house wreckers to see how much they'd bid for the materials in the place. Ordinarily, as I've pointed out, Nantucketers are extremely thrifty. They approve of efforts to salvage anything, including bent nails, which can be straightened and used again. But in the case of The Shoe, each of the house wreckers decided that even the nails had had it.

I was secretly pleased to know that if I had had the nerve to express my earlier opinion about high bids on the house wrecking, I could now say, "I told you so"—if I dared to.

Bob placed such an exaggerated sentimental value on The Shoe that he had difficulty in accepting the premise that it had no intrinsic value. He kept insisting, with more loyalty than logic, that if the house wreckers knew their jobs, they'd realize that the sagging beams were seasoned and sturdy and that, under the flaking whitewash of the interior, there were "genuine antique doors" and "priceless woodwork."

Becoming increasingly irritated because his professional judgment had been questioned, one house wrecker finally announced:

"If it was my place, boys, I'd first remove all the genuwine antique doors and all the genuwine priceless woodwork. I wouldn't trust no house wrecker with *that* job. I'd mind that they didn't get scratched, and put them careful in a pile in the back yard."

"You would?" Bob asked eagerly.

"Bet your life. And then I wouldn't bother to call no house wrecker. You're big fellows, all three of you. Why don't the three of you go up on the roof and jump up and down just once?"

"Maybe," I said, thinking I could relieve some of Bob's disappointment by making one of my tactful little jokes, "they could get that wolf from the story about the three little pigs. You know, the wolf who huffed and puffed and huffed and puffed, and blew the house down."

I laughed and so did the house wrecker. I think Bob's mother wanted to laugh, too, because I'm sure she appreciates as much as I do the humor of her sons all taking over her affairs on such occasions. She gave me a quick, understanding glance over the top of her glasses, and went back to a manuscript she was writing in longhand on her lap.

"Don't you think, Barbara," Frank inquired coldly, "you are rather crabbing this gentleman's act—that one comedian on the premises at a time is sufficient?"

"That wolf, Mrs. Anchor, wouldn't have to bother with no puffs nor the second huff neither," the house wrecker informed me with obvious approval. "Just that first huff, and Katy, bar the door. You'd *see* the place go down!"

He laughed again, this time slapping his knee. I couldn't help but join in.

"All right, all right, maybe the house isn't any good," Bob said impatiently. He swallowed the bait. "But how about those doors and woodwork you said we should pile carefully in the back yard."

"Oh, yes, I near forgot about them," said the house wrecker, now enjoying himself immensely. "You want to rub them down good with kerosene and then set fire to them."

He exploded in mirth, and again I couldn't help but join him. This time, I could almost have sworn I heard a choking gurgle from Bob's mother, but when I looked her way she was still writing busily on the manuscript.

The house wrecker departed, and another bulletin was sent out to the other members of the family. The Shoe was not worth salvaging.

There followed round-table family discussions on Nantucket, conferences in Montclair, seminars on the West Coast, long-distance phone calls, and the sketching of eleven different sets of proposed house plans.

Also, at one time or another, architects in Nantucket, San Francisco, Boston, New York and Lafayette, Indiana, were consulted to see if they would like the all-important job of drawing up plans for the cottage, which was supposed to cost ten thousand dollars. I have to give Bob's family credit for one thing: When it sets out on a project which involves (a) money and (b) tradition, it not only looks before it leaps but gets down on its knees and microscopically examines the terrain for a distance of several thousand miles.

Characteristically, after the ground had been examined, a decision was reached firmly, efficiently and expeditiously.

They'd forget all the planning they had done and get a prefabricated house.

I never have understood how that decision was reached, but I have my suspicions. I think that someone or other, confronted with eleven different sketches of house plans, chose the psychologist's way out of a dilemma. Since the someone or other to whom I refer is also a motion-study expert, it seems probable to me that she might also have made up her own mind—right at the very start—that there would be price advantages to a prefabricated house.

In any event, the decision, once made, seemed unanimous. To this day Bob believes that he was the one who first advised his mother to put up a prefabricated new Shoe. Several of his brothers also claim this distinction. Once, when Bob asked his mother to confirm the fact that the idea had been his, she replied with a perfectly straight face:

"As I recall, dear, you boys all told me about prefabs, at about the same time."

So perhaps that's the way it was. Accepting her statement at face value, one would have to assume that she knew little or nothing about the existence of prefabs, until her sons told her about them. This is a broad assumption in view of the fact that, over a period of several years, she had had business connections with a large Indiana firm which specializes in prefabs. One would also have to assume that it was merely a coincidence that this same firm was selected to manufacture the new Shoe.

The firm did a wonderful job of it, too, adapting one of its standard models to conform with the weather-shingled Nantucket architecture, and at the same time to match the basic floor plan of the old Shoe.

I've gone into all of this in some detail because the new Shoe was built for year-around living and Anchor Inn wasn't. As Bob and I had suspected, the rumor mill proved accurate about the social science teacher. He resigned and Bob was quickly hired. And since Bob's family intended to use the new Shoe only in the summer, that meant we could live in it during the winter.

Obviously, it was an ideal arrangement for us. Or at any rate, that's what we thought it was going to be.

15 ~ Curtain for Charade

Until Bob became a teacher at the high school and we were accepted as members of the community, we had only the vaguest sort of ideas—usually erroneous—about the off-season life on the island.

It's true, we had seen Nantucket in the early spring. But then we were still treated as visitors; as members of the audience rather than as members of the cast.

Now, as the curtain came down on the summer's final charade, a surprising transformation of characters began to take place. For us, the transformation was sometimes disillusioning and sometimes just the opposite.

Take, for instance, a bearded old-timer who is a summertime fixture on Main Street, where he sits on a bench under the elms and whittles. With his white curls showing beneath his oilskin cap and with his corncob pipe cocked jauntily in the corner of his mouth, he is the embodiment of the retired seafaring man. His likeness must decorate the pages of thousands of albums, because the one-day excursionists—known as "trippers"—photograph him almost continuously during the daylight hours. Even the regular summer visitors often address him respectfully as "Cap'n," and feel pleased when he returns their greetings. He'll fix his sharp, humor-filled eyes on the sky and predict the weather for you, if you ask him politely. And sometimes, in a quarter-deck voice, he'll spin you a yarn about the sea.

Well, maybe he *is* an old sea captain—I don't know. But I do know that he isn't a Nantucketer. When the last of the tourists are departing, he departs, too—for his home in a suburb of New York.

When the tourists left, a summertime doctor—and a good one—started getting his boat ready for his rugged winter-time business as a scalloper. He still practiced medicine now and then in the winter, but the scallops were his main source of revenue. His summer patients probably wouldn't have recognized the wind-chapped, disheveled shell fisherman, clad in rubber boots and mackinaw, as he guided his dirty motorboat up to her berth, kicked the engine into neutral, and stepped nimbly forward to secure the bow line.

It required a certain amount of adjusting, when I'd pass a woman schoolteacher on the street that autumn, to think of her as a colleague of Bob's and not as the girl who mixes ice cream and tonic at the drug store; or as the girl at the stamp window at the post office; or as the girl who drives the bus to the beach.

A man whom I had catalogued, on the basis of his summer job, as Rubbish Truck Driver had to be re-catalogued as Big Local Politician. Beauty Parlor Assistant became Large Property Holder. Ticket Agent became School Board Chairman.

It took some adjusting for Bob, too, because practically every teacher on Nantucket has a summer business or job.

Even the superintendent rented rooms to summer visitors. So did the principal of the high school.

Most of the teachers rented rooms, clerked in stores, drove taxis and buses, or took tourists fishing. One teacher was a summertime deliveryman for a liquor store. Another was a carpenter. Another pumped gas for a filling station. Another was a receptionist for an osteopath.

Summer residents might be surprised to learn that many of the Nantucketers whom they hire to do manual and menial jobs are actually cultivated and intelligent persons. I think that some of the intelligent Nantucketers rather enjoy posing in the summertime as rustics, and purposely fall back on "ain'ts," double negatives, and "wal I calc'lates."

Many summer residents also hold firmly to the irate belief that the relatively high prices of groceries and other goods on Nantucket are designed deliberately to separate off-islanders from the maximum amount of vacation money in the minimum time.

They believe—and Bob and I also used to suspect—that there are two sets of summertime prices: A high set for the visitors, who had better be milked while the milking is good; and a low set for the natives, who presumably get discounts or under-the-counter refunds when the tourists aren't looking.

Bob and I waited hopefully that autumn for prices to come down. We felt sure that, no matter how closely guarded the secret, it would be impossible for the merchants to maintain and even to advertise a high set of prices especially for us, while giving the discounts or refunds to everybody else.

We also thought that, once we were in on the secret, we would be eligible for future summer discounts.

"If we ever find out how the racket really works," I had assured Bob, "they'll have to give us the lower prices next summer. Otherwise, we would spill the beans."

The fact is that prices don't come down in the winter. If anything, they edge up, because the volume of business drops off sharply.

And of course there is only one set of prices in the summer. In saying this, I realize that some skeptical summer visitors will nod their heads sagely and conclude that Bob and I have been let in on the secret and are now a part of an island-wide conspiracy to defraud them.

Nevertheless, the sole reason for high prices, both in winter and summer, is high freight rates. Since the steamers are subsidized by the Commonwealth of Massachusetts, and still lose money, the high freight rates can't be blamed on anyone, either.

Bob and I soon moved into the new Shoe, which, as almost any Nantucketer could tell you, had an all-electric kitchen, including automatic washing machine and dish-washer.

Since Bob's family couldn't bear to part with the two lighthouses, they were left standing and the new cottage was erected between them. The old Shoe, except for those portions Bob reserved for kindling wood, was carted away to the dump.

There was, to say the least, a marked contrast between the old Shoe and the new. Still, Bob seldom allowed me to forget that the old structure, however dilapidated, had certain advantages which modern engineering had failed to duplicate.

"When you swept the kitchen of the *old* Shoe," he pointed out, "you didn't have to bother with a dustpan. The sand would go right through the cracks and the knotholes in the floorboards.

"And for another thing, how are we going to see whether Ann is growing as fast as my sisters did when they were her age, now that the doorway with all the height marks on it is gone?"

Also, it was impossible for Bob to start an open fire in the living room without identifying the precise source of each stick of kindling wood.

"See that?" he'd tell me excitedly, holding forth an eight-inch splinter. "See that? Now I want to test your powers of observation. Where did *that* come from?"

"The old Shoe," I'd say, going along with the formula.

"That's right. But the point is *where? Where* in the old Shoe?"

"I don't know."

"See those three spots of black paint? That was part of the Morse code on the bathroom wall, don't you remember? It sat right about *this* high from the floor. It was part of the letter 'H.' "

"I remember, honey," I'd tell him patiently.

"A shame," Bob would sigh, relegating that particular piece of kindling to the fireplace and carefully studying another piece. "A shame."

After the novelty wore off the new Shoe and after I had succeeded in recataloguing my Nantucket acquaintances, I was plunged into a sense of depression which is difficult to explain.

I don't pretend to speak for islanders, but it's my impression that they, too, feel let down, restless, and isolated as the summer season ends and they're left to face the long winter with only themselves for company. In the old days, "wadgetty" was the word used on Nantucket for nervous irritability. That's how I felt as the weather turned gray and dismal and as I got more and more tired of seeing the same people day after day. Mighty wadgetty!

The sense of depression is brought on, I think, by the awareness that one has been left behind in a general, lively exodus for greener pastures. Not only the summer residents but many of the more enterprising Nantucketers pull up stakes. And those who are left must mark time, figuratively taking in each other's washing, with nothing to look forward to but town meetin', till next summer's influx.

So when I looked out of the windows of the new Shoe and saw the bathing beaches drab and deserted, I got an empty ache in the pit of my stomach. The bathhouses were boarded up, and purple lines of seaweed had replaced the beach umbrellas on the shore. The hard-surfaced parking lots, where roadsters and station wagons had sat bumper to bumper, now became the property of seagulls. Carrying mussels they had pried from the jetty rocks and gathered from the beach, the birds flew over the parking lots at a height of about thirty feet, and broke open the mussels by dropping them on the pavement. This was exciting to watch for the first few days and interesting to watch for the first few weeks. But as time went on it became sort of boring!

The Shoe has a clear view of the bathing beaches, but is ringed in the back by a semicircle of summer houses, in a low-lying meadow under the Cliff. These were vacant now, and all activity was centered in the village, three-quarters of a mile away. Our feeling of isolation was heightened by rains and snow which flooded the meadow right up to—and often including—The Shoe's basement.

The sun sometimes failed to put in an appearance for days at a time, as an unbelievably bone-chilling fog bank hung over the Atlantic. On those occasions when the sun did manage to come through, it usually had a blue-white cast, so bright it caused your eyes to water, but containing no real warmth. A howling, shutter-rattling wind blew in over the bathing beaches most of the time, peppering the house with sand and forming new dunes in the front yard. We finally had to stop using the front door, in order to prevent the dunes from forming in the living room.

Even with the front door shut, staying in the new Shoe was a little like spending the winter in a frigid sand storm. Although the windows fit snugly and were weatherstripped, the sand managed to get in. After a windy night, Ann could write her name with her finger on the furniture in the living room. You could feel the sand between the sheets in bed, and you had to rinse out the tub before taking a bath.

The gusty nights were especially nerve-racking, and I would have felt better if we had had some neighbors for company. The wind pinged sand against our windows and played "Moaning Low" around the two lighthouses. And the jetties' fog horn sang the blues out there in the spindrift. How does the song go—"I've got a right to sing the blues; I've got a right to feel low down?" No fog horn ever had a better right!

I suppose it can be argued that a nature-lover would like Nantucket best in winter, when the beaches and the moors aren't cluttered up with bathers and picnickers. But as I faced and refaced the gray nakedness of our beach, I discovered that a little nature goes a long way.

Bob and I both found that there was something claustrophobic about seeing the same faces day after day, with the sure knowledge that we would never—or hardly ever—see a *different* face. It wasn't long before we got to know the face of everyone on the island. Shortly after that, we got to know the faces of almost all the dogs and cats. I finally got to the point where I sometimes thought I could recognize the various seagulls.

I was fortunate enough to be taken into a sewing club and a rug-making club, both composed of agreeable young women. We met around at each other's houses and really had a grand time swapping stories about our summer roomers and scooping the local weeklies on printable and unprintable news. If a few of *our* summer guests had been odd, they couldn't begin to match some of the guests my fellow club members told about. My story of the man who collected rocks went over pretty well, but even *I* had to admit it didn't hold a candle to one about a nude male sleep-walker who seemed intent on finding a secret panel in a staircase, or one about a female alcoholic who prowled around on tiptoe in the early morning hours searching for liquor in the rooms of other guests.

At these club meetings, I was also introduced to Nantucket cooking, which I think compares favorably to any in the world. The refreshments, modestly referred to as "collations," often consisted of sandwiches, hot breads, home-made pickles, beach-plum preserves, delicious flaky pies, shortcake, and hand-churned ice cream.

Along with the talking and eating, we club members even found time to do a certain amount of sewing and rug-making.

As a matter of fact there were plenty of attractive, interesting people on Nantucket. Bob and I fell in with a congenial group, and we got together every so often to talk, drink wine, and dance to the radio. There were some married teachers and their spouses; the editor of one of the newspapers and his wife who was his star reporter and who kept an alert ear tuned to the reports of the rumor mill; a wonderfully kind and competent and outspoken spinster-astronomer whose special project is to keep tabs on Eros, a variable asteroid; a young mainlander who spends the winters in a one-man project of converting huge old summer houses into two smaller summer houses, with modern conveniences. (He begins a conversion project simply by climbing with a handsaw onto the roof of one of the big three-story shingled "cottages"— constructed in the days of large families, small income taxes, and armies of servants—and sawing the building in two. After the sawing is completed, he has a moving crew help him to separate the two halves by about eighteen inches. Then he uses one half as the scaffolding to put a new outside wall on the other half.)

Such people were stimulating. Their presence helped the winter months to pass more quickly. Without them, I might very well have gone stir-crazy. But I hope they will excuse me for saying that, especially during the extremely wadgetty months of January and February, there were times when I didn't care if I never saw their faces again. I'm sure they felt the same way about *my* face and, for that matter, so did I.

Our claustrophobia was aggravated by the knowledge that there was no place to go to escape the familiar faces. On the mainland, if you live in a city, you can step out of your apartment and immediately become lost in the crowd. If you live in a small town, you can climb into your car on Sunday afternoon and ride as far as you want.

Bob and I have always been Sunday afternoon drivers. When we lived in Bloomfield, we used to like to ride around aimlessly looking at houses and discovering new suburbs and new country roads. There's a close, secure, married feeling in being alone with your husband while driving through unexplored territory peopled by strangers. You don't have to watch your manners, or care much how you look, or be alert to wave and smile at someone. If you have an urge to be impolite, you can point out an outlandish hat to your husband and laugh out loud—it doesn't matter; the woman doesn't know you from Adam, you're already a block away from her, and you'll never see her again.

On Nantucket, you will see everybody tomorrow, or within a few days. You can never drive aimlessly, because there are only a few places to go and the roads aim directly at them. When you reach those places, on an island twelve miles long and four miles wide, you will find acquaintances who are also trying to escape from the same old faces. Many of them will be interesting, cultivated people, but for the moment you don't want to see them and they don't want to see you. Yet you must smile, you must roll down the window on your side of the car and exchange pleasantries.

There is no such thing as being lost in a crowd on wintertime Nantucket. You must always be a part of the crowd, and the crowd itself is not very large.

It sometimes got me down.

16 ~ Professor Fatcat

"Teaching school here," Bob once remarked to me in academic tones while correcting a stack of English themes, "is sometimes rather a challenge."

He was right about that. And while on the subject of challenges, I challenge anyone to match that remark for understatement. I don't mean to imply that Nantucket children are "bad" or even difficult. But they *are* "independent," and so much so that no school teacher there has a very easy time, particularly during his first year.

As one school official once told me, when we were having a friendly discussion about the matter at a party:

"No Nantucket child will ever grow up into a citizen who is ripe to be taken over by a dictator."

He got no argument from me. In fact, I'd pity the dictator who ever made the mistake of trying it.

Innside Nantucket

The Nantucket youngster comes honestly by his love of independence and his suspicion of meddlesome authority—particularly off-island authority. Nantucketers historically have made their own livings in spite of, rather than because of, rules laid down by off-island officials. Tariffs, smuggling laws, restrictions on salvaging goods from wrecked vessels, embargoes, fishing regulations all bite into the incomes of seafaring people.

Nantucket was settled by first-generation Americans whose parents had left Britain precisely because of hatred for fettering regulations. As I mentioned before, the Boston Tea Party, staged in resentment against British taxes, occurred on Nantucket ships. The whaling captains whose schooners roamed the world became accustomed to being a law unto themselves. Their wives, left at home to run things, experienced an independence known to few women of the Nineteenth Century. Perhaps this explains why the Women's Suffrage movement got such an early start on Nantucket.

Today's Nantucketer is law-abiding in the extreme when it comes to important matters with which he's in agreement. He sees the sense in laws against murder, rape, arson, and theft, and complies with them. On relatively trivial matters, with which he disagrees, his attitude is often a cheerful, "Well, I'd like to see someone aim to stop me."

Bossy people themselves, Nantucketers cling to a horror of being bossed. They strongly suspect that all duly elected or appointed officials—including school teachers—soon will be too big for their breeches.

This suspicion is particularly strong as it affects off-islanders. Although Bob's salary was only twenty-five hundred dollars a year —the same, incidentally as the high school janitor's—some Nantucketers seemed to think that this amounted to wallowing at the public trough. I'm afraid a few of them regarded Bob as a tax-eating fatcat. They didn't see any justice at all in our having an inn, a new station wagon, and use of a cottage with an all-electric kitchen—plus a public job paying the round sum of twenty-five hundred dollars.

Since many of these Nantucketers had to struggle through the winters without any salaries at all, we could well understand their viewpoint. I will say, though, that Bob earned every penny of his salary.

We could also understand their viewpoint when it came to breaking minor regulations. For instance, a local health ordinance says that garbage must be collected and burned. It's probably a sensible ordinance, but you have to pay a fee to get your garbage picked up. Since many Nantucketers don't have wintertime jobs, they can't afford to pay the fee. Consequently, they carry their garbage out to the dump.

Town officials, recognizing the need for leniency and both recognizing and sharing the distrust of too much authority, usually don't try to enforce unimportant or unpopular laws.

Scalloping rules are generally observed mostly when the scallops are plentiful. When they are scarce, the reasoning is that a man has to make a living, regardless of laws thought up by land-lubbers who wouldn't know a scallop from a quahaug. The same applies to the hunting season, although here the reasoning is that a man is entitled to a certain amount of sport on an island where sporting activities are far from numerous.

A number of Nantucket townspeople, shrugging off repeated warnings by officials, kept hens pecking away in the back yards of their homes, despite laws saying that hens couldn't be kept within the town. And one marvelously independent woman defied the selectmen, the police, and a court order by keeping in her house nine more dogs than the legal limit of three. She said she'd take a gun to any busybody who tried to come after her "doggies."

A good portion of the community backed her stand, on grounds that she was fighting a battle for all of them.

"If you let some Meddlesome Mattie tell you that you can only have three dogs," one of the girls in my rug club explained to me, "the next thing you know, somebody will be telling you that you can't have any dogs at all—or that you can't have more than three children."

A former selectman once said that, "Some of the laws of Massachusetts stop at Tuckernuck." Tuckernuck is a small island off the western tip of Nantucket, and thus is between Nantucket and the mainland. The selectman might have gone a little farther and said that some of the laws of Nantucket stop at the old plastered walls of the Selectmen's Chamber.

Of course, a rugged individual who thinks that anyone on the public payroll may soon become too big for his breeches usually passes this belief along to his children. If a boy's father says that no fatcat politician is going to tell him when he has to stop scalloping, and if a boy's mother says that no ward-heeler is going to tell her she can't keep chickens, the boy is liable to say that no tax-eating school teacher is going to tell him that he mustn't whisper or blow bubbles with his chewing gum.

On the day Bob started teaching, I was up town doing the marketing when I got a report on what *used* to go on at the high school.

"So Bawb's up at the high school, eh?" a middle-aged chap whom I knew slightly asked me in the grocery store. "I guess you haven't heard yet how he's getting along."

"It's only the first day of school," I pointed out. "I hope he's getting along well."

222

"When I was a kid in high school," he guffawed, "we had a helluva time—especially with the new teachers. We used to like to see how long they'd last. If you could get rid of enough of them, you could get out of some classes."

He guffawed again, and I hoped my facial expressions didn't show how little I was enjoying the conversation.

"One teacher went away for Columbus Day weekend, and never came back. And there was another cute little trick who tried to keep some of us in after school. We brought a bunch of beer bottles, and rolled them up the aisle at her. Kept her dodging, too."

"Why, that was terrible!" I protested.

"Sure was," he agreed, still laughing. "But, you know, boys will be boys."

Before I got home that day, I received other first-hand reports of similar merriment at the high school, in bygone days. A woman told me that one of her teachers had become so aggravated that she'd told the class if they didn't behave she'd throw their beautifully decorated Christmas tree out of the window. When they still didn't behave, she carried out her threat and then stood there at the open window to see if anyone wanted to follow the tree.

Still another teacher, I was told, had made an example of a boy who had sassed her once too often. She dangled him out the window by one leg until he apologized.

"I'm sure the children aren't as bad as that!" I protested.

"They're angels compared with what we were, I reckon," my informant said.

I felt as if I ought to get out the first-aid kit, in preparation for Bob's return, but when he finally got home that night he was unmarked and not too discouraged.

When I asked him if anything had been thrown at him, he looked at me with a puzzled frown, and then replied:

"No! Say, who have you been talking to, anyway?"

"Just a few of the alumni," I sighed.

Nantucket's isolation, insofar as some of its residents are concerned, was brought home to us by the fact that a number of children in the elementary school had never been off-island. That meant they had never seen a city, a building more than three stories high, a railroad train, a circus, a three-lane highway, or a traffic light. Occasionally a civic group in Boston will entertain four or five children who have never before been off-island. These trips prove to be an eye-opener not only for the children but for their hosts as well.

Even in the high school, where Bob taught, there are quite a few freshmen and sophomores who had been off-island only once or twice, and then perhaps only to New Bedford and Fall River.

I used to get all choked up when I'd see the boys on the high-school football team, glowing with excitement but trying to appear blasé as if it were an everyday affair, prepare to embark for a game on the mainland.

One classroom incident also served to illustrate the island's isolation at least in regard to a particular matter. Besides social studies, Bob also taught a couple of English classes. In one of these, he read aloud a poem about the death of Sam McGee. When he got to that part of the poem in which the aforesaid Mr. McGee was laid to rest in a coffin, he was interrupted by a raised hand.

"What's a coffin, Mr. Gilbreth?" asked one of the children—and, mind you, this was *high school!*

"Why," said Bob, "a coffin is a casket. It's something you put dead people in. Certainly you know that."

This brought a number of incredulous stares, and finally a roar of amusement at the expense of three Coffin children in the class. On Nantucket, the Coffins and the Folgers outnumber the Smiths. Both Coffins and Folgers are old and respected whaling families. Lucretia Mott, the Quaker minister and suffragette was a Nantucket Coffin. Benjamin Franklin's mother was a Nantucket Folger.

I suppose that, out of deference to the many holders of the Coffin surname, Nantucketers some time back stopped using the common noun as a synonym of casket. In any event, the non-Coffins in the class were intrigued and immensely pleased to learn that the surname could also be spelled with a small "c." And Bob felt guilty about having passed along information on a subject which appeared to be taboo.

In another English class, Bob told his pupils that they should each read a book and hand in reports. He had not been very well satisfied with the reading habits of the children, and he was particularly gratified when one girl asked:

"Would it be all right if I give a book report on a *Classic?*"

"It would not only be all right," he assured her, "it would be splendid."

Bob was so pleased with her fine example that, when the reports came due two weeks later, he singled her out to read her paper aloud to the class. To his additional gratification and amazement, the classic which she had selected turned out to be Victor Hugo's best-known work. For five minutes, Bob sat wide-eyed while he listened to the girl recount accurately and graphically the story of *Les Miserables*. When she had finished, Bob was lavish with his praise. "That was a grand account of the book," he told her, "and I'm certainly pleased that you tackled such a long volume and understood the book so thoroughly."

"Oh, I didn't read the book, Mr. Gilbreth," she told him—and she wasn't being fresh but merely stating a fact—"I read the *Classic.*"

Bob didn't understand. "Isn't the classic the book?" he asked. "Or, at any rate, isn't the book a classic? Of course it is."

"I don't know about that," she insisted, "but I read the *Classic.*"

She then opened her notebook and pulled out a comic-book volume of a series entitled *Classic.* It contained a picture story of *Les Miserables.*

"Do you mean to tell me that you've given a report on a *comic* book?" Bob inquired. "I can't accept a book report on that!"

"Why can't you?" she replied, on the verge of righteous tears. "I asked you if I could read a *Classic,* and you said 'yes.' You said 'splendid.'" She turned to the class. "Didn't he?"

The class agreed to a Nantucketer that that was exactly what Bob had said.

So, all right, let me be the first to concede that the same lack of knowledge about the classics can probably be found in any American high school. I come to praise Nantucket, not to bury it in any—well—casket.

Let me also concede that the Nantucket youngster, in spite of and perhaps because of his distaste for being "bossed," may grow up to be a more valuable citizen than his mainland contemporary.

That doesn't change the fact that Nantucket children, as Bob put it, sometimes are a challenge to their teachers.

A real challenge. And since Bob is still in the teaching profession and concerned with professional ethics, I shall say no more!

17 ~ Return of the Native

In August, after our second winter on the island, Bob accepted a better position as social studies teacher and building principal in Franklin, New Hampshire.

We were expecting our second child that same month. We planned to close Anchor Inn early in September and move to Franklin.

Most of August passed and, somewhat to Bob's annoyance, the baby still hadn't arrived. Although Bob didn't say it in so many words, he implied rather strongly that punctuality was a virtue with which I had not been overly endowed.

"I know it's not your fault, honey," he told me, "and I don't agree with husbands who think that a woman's having a baby is any picnic. But can't you see that it would be a lot easier for all of us if you'd go ahead and get it over with?

"I have no use," he informed me on another occasion, "for men who expect their wives to act like Indian squaws, when it comes to having babies. As you no doubt know . . ."

"You told me twice before," I interrupted him. "The squaws, on a cross-country march, would drop out of line, have their papooses, and rejoin the march a few minutes later. Well, I'm no squaw!"

"Who said you were?" Bob protested. "Didn't I just get through saying I didn't have any use for men who expected their wives to have their babies that way?"

"Just don't bring it up, then," I suggested.

"I'll swear, women expecting babies certainly do get irritable," Bob complained. "Anyway, you *will* have to admit that procrastination is the thief of time."

When unoriginal remarks such as these failed to shame me into getting down to the serious business at hand, Bob decided to switch to jocularity.

"Well, Barb," he said gaily one morning, "do you know what today is?"

"Labor Day," I admitted.

"And does that suggest anything to you, honey?"

"Much as I want to drop out of line and have this papoose," I threatened, "if I hear one more word out of you about her, I'll carry her until Washington's Birthday."

" 'Her!' " replied Bob. "That shows how much *you* know!"

Labor Day passed and Bob had to go to Franklin to assume his new position. Because the baby was now expected daily, it was hardly feasible to move the whole family to Franklin. But as I packed Bob's suitcase, I complained:

"It's going to be dismal here without you, especially having the baby without you to pace the floor. I wish I were going, too."

"Look, honey," said Bob, picking me up and sitting me down

228

on his lap—which was no mean feat of strength in view of my condition, "we'd better get something straightened out. You can come to Franklin right now, if you want to. But I thought . . . Well, this one's probably going to be a boy. Everyone says so, isn't that right?"

"It's right that everybody says so," I nodded sadly.

"Well, don't you want our son to be born on *Nantucket?* It's Tradition! You wouldn't want him to be born on the *mainland,* would you?"

I thought this over. I didn't care particularly where he or she would be born, if only he or she would hurry up and get it over with. But Bob's explanation threw a new light on matters. If Bob felt that strongly about it. . . .

"All right," I agreed. "I'll stay. I can't guarantee the sex, but I'll guarantee you a Nantucketer."

And so Roy was born on Nantucket. He thoughtfully chose a weekend, with Bob flying down for the occasion, and informing me proudly that he had known all along I could do it, if I'd put my mind on it.

When I finally boarded the steamer for the mainland, I felt almost as if I were shedding chains. Yet I couldn't help shedding a few tears as the familiar landfalls fell astern. My emotions were so mixed that I didn't even remember about the tradition of dropping a penny at Brant Point.

It is difficult to describe, but I found my wintertime attitude toward Nantucket changing almost as soon as I reached the mainland. I missed the moors' pungent smell; the clean yellow sands; the cobblestone paving; the sturdy old homes where a hundred sea captains once lived in a row; the winding lanes with the fascinating names of Petticoat Row, Easy Street, Hussey, Tattle Court, Whalers Lane, Vesper Lane, Darling; the rutted roads that swing through sanddunes to deserted miles of beach, where the surf pulses the heartbeat of the sea.

That's right; I wanted to go back. And so did Bob and Ann. Not in the winter, because we had had enough of that; but when the mayflowers are in bloom; when the broom is wearing its startling yellow; when the rambler roses are flowering in tumbled profusion on the walls and roofs of the fishing shacks in Sconset; when the sun cuts early through the pre-dawn mist to warm a west wind scented with three thousand miles of ocean.

We wanted to go back when the fly-specked newspapers had been taken down from the windows of the closed shops, when the makeshift shutters had been removed, when Nantucketers were so busy working that they didnt have time to get in each other's hair—or we in theirs.

We wanted to go back. Once again, we began counting the days.

In late spring, I went on ahead of Bob—who still had a few more weeks of school—to get things started at Anchor Inn. I took Roy and Ann with me, because Bob couldn't very well look out for them and teach school at the same time.

I thought I could smell the moors almost as soon as the steamer left Woods Hole. The weather was warm, and the ocean incredibly blue and beautiful.

I got a stateroom for the children, but I had trouble keeping Ann in it. Roy went to sleep shortly after we left Martha's Vineyard, and I suddenly became aware that Ann had been missing for some time. I went out on deck to look for her, but couldn't immediately find her. Finally, when I had finished searching the top deck and was beginning to become concerned, I heard her voice up forward, near the bridge.

I went up there, past a chain with a "No Admittance" sign, and found her standing with legs spread apart and hands clasped behind her back, keeping a sharp weather-eye on the horizon.

"When we come up to the Cross Rip Lightship," she ordered, imitating Bob, "I want one blast on the whistle and I want you to swing her helm sharply to starboard. Look alive, now!"

"Aye-aye, sir," gravely replied a man with "Captain" written on his cap.

Seeing me, he asked: "Is this your daughter, Mrs. Anchor?"

"I'm sorry," I said. "I'll get her out of your way."

"*Another* Gilbreth kid," he sighed, "and darn near ready to take examinations for her pilot's license."